JUMBLE®

Anniversary

65 Years of Jumbles!

Henri Arnold,
Bob Lee,
Jeff Knurek, &
David L. Hoyt

TRIUMPH
BOOKS

For further information, contact:
Triumph Books LLC
814 North Franklin Street
Chicago, Illinois 60610
Phone: (312) 337-0747
www.triumphbooks.com

Printed in U.S.A.
ISBN: 978-1-62937-734-6

Design by Sue Knopf

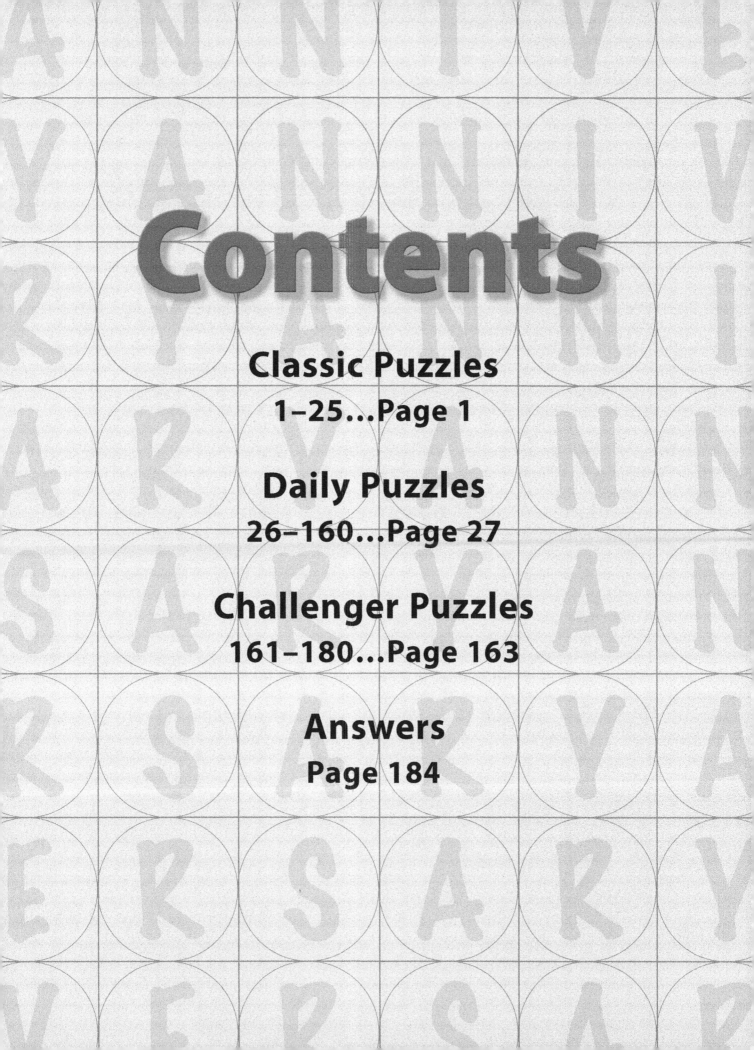

Contents

JUMBLE®

Anniversary

Classic
Puzzles

JUMBLE®

Unscramble these four Jumbles, one letter
to each square, to form four ordinary words.

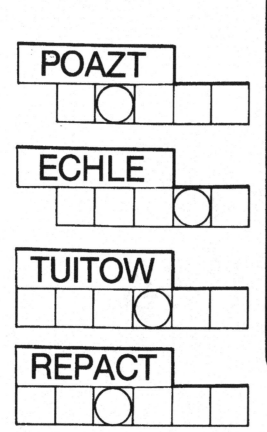

POAZT

ECHLE

TUITOW

REPACT

WHAT THE GUY WHO
SWORE HE WAS GO-
ING TO LOSE WEIGHT
ENDED UP EATING.

Now arrange the circled letters to form
the surprise answer, as suggested by the
above cartoon.

Print answer here "  "

JUMBLE

Unscramble these four Jumbles, one letter to each square, to form four ordinary words.

YOOTS

TOISH

FUPULC

TOMSED

At this rate, we'll be nabbed before we finish the job

WHAT A CAT BURGLAR MUST NEVER DO.

Now arrange the circled letters to form the surprise answer, as suggested by the above cartoon.

Print answer here

3

JUMBLE®

Unscramble these four Jumbles, one letter to each square, to form four ordinary words.

FEZOR

WOYNS

GAHOME

CEETIN

DELICATESSEN

CAVIAR PATÉ TRUFFLES

SAID WITH A SMILE.

Now arrange the circled letters to form the surprise answer, as suggested by the above cartoon.

Print answer here

JUMBLE®

Unscramble these four Jumbles, one letter
to each square, to form four ordinary words.

DORIF

PAMCH

GRENED

BONECK

WHAT THAT OLD
GOAT ACTED LIKE.

Now arrange the circled letters to form
the surprise answer, as suggested by the
above cartoon.

Print answer here ◯ " ◯◯◯ "

JUMBLE®

Unscramble these four Jumbles, one letter to each square, to form four ordinary words.

GLOIC

RAGUD

GOCHUR

VECIED

Cheap

WHEN SHE SAID I COULD MAKE HER "MINE," I KNEW SHE WAS THIS

Now arrange the circled letters to form the surprise answer, as suggested by the above cartoon.

Print answer here " A ☐☐☐☐☐ ☐☐☐☐☐☐☐ "

JUMBLE®

Unscramble these four Jumbles, one letter
to each square, to form four ordinary words.

ROARB

TUFOL

URAUBE

KOTLEC

IF YOU'RE SUFFERING
FROM LARYNGITIS,
YOU'D BEST NOT
DO THIS.

Now arrange the circled letters to form
the surprise answer, as suggested by the
above cartoon.

Print answer here ⬡⬡⬡⬡ ⬡⬡⬡⬡⬡ IT

JUMBLE®

Unscramble these four Jumbles, one letter to each square, to form four ordinary words.

GUNTS

OGGRE

HUBLES

WAHELI

Nice day

It'll probably rain

THE PESSIMIST HUNG AROUND THE DELI-CATESSEN LOOKING FOR THIS.

Now arrange the circled letters to form the surprise answer, as suggested by the above cartoon.

Print answer here   THE " ⬡⬡⬡⬡⬡ "

JUMBLE®

Unscramble these four Jumbles, one letter
to each square, to form four ordinary words.

PERAP

KOBOR

VERREE

LUCASE

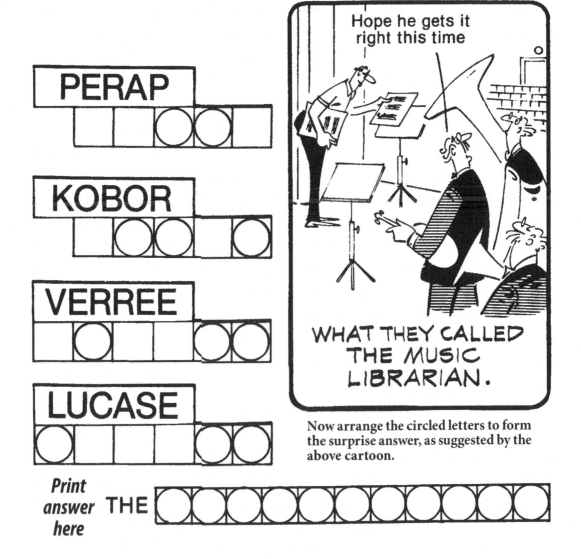

Hope he gets it
right this time

WHAT THEY CALLED
THE MUSIC
LIBRARIAN.

Now arrange the circled letters to form
the surprise answer, as suggested by the
above cartoon.

Print
answer THE
here

JUMBLE.

Unscramble these four Jumbles, one letter
to each square, to form four ordinary words.

UCLID

MASCH

ONBOAB

QUIETY

Oh, dear

SHOULD YOU CUT
THEM AND THROW
THEM AWAY— OR
JUST FILE THEM?

Now arrange the circled letters to form
the surprise answer, as suggested by the
above cartoon.

Print answer here

JUMBLE®

Unscramble these four Jumbles, one letter
to each square, to form four ordinary words.

POVER

THOLC

CRASAF

TREEMP

WHAT THAT TV
SHOW ABOUT SKIING
TURNED OUT TO BE.

Now arrange the circled letters to form
the surprise answer, as suggested by the
above cartoon.

Print
answer A " ⚬⚬⚬⚬⚬ " ⚬⚬⚬⚬⚬
here

○○○○○○○○○○○○○ ○○○○○○○○○○○○○○○

JUMBLE®

Unscramble these four Jumbles, one letter
to each square, to form four ordinary words.

UNDOP

HASUQ

UNGOLE

NARFIA

WHAT THEY CALLED
THE BEAUTICIAN.

Now arrange the circled letters to form
the surprise answer, as suggested by the
above cartoon.

Print
answer   THE "◯◯◯ — ◯◯◯◯◯◯◯◯"
here

JUMBLE®

Unscramble these four Jumbles, one letter to each square, to form four ordinary words.

FREVE

ALYMN

YARBEK

THELAH

WHAT THEY CALLED THAT CLASSY NEW ART GALLERY.

Now arrange the circled letters to form the surprise answer, as suggested by the above cartoon.

Print answer here THE ☐☐☐☐☐ OF ☐☐☐☐☐☐

JUMBLE®

Unscramble these four Jumbles, one letter
to each square, to form four ordinary words.

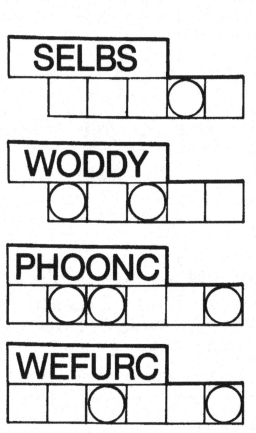

SELBS

WODDY

PHOONC

WEFURC

WHAT THE KID WHO
SAID HE DIDN'T
LIKE ALPHABET SOUP
ENDED UP EATING.

Now arrange the circled letters to form
the surprise answer, as suggested by the
above cartoon.

Print answer here HIS ☐☐☐ ☐☐☐☐☐

JUMBLE®

Unscramble these four Jumbles, one letter
to each square, to form four ordinary words.

TYTUP

TASID

OANNEY

DRAMOR

WHAT THE INVISIBLE
MAN'S MOTHER OR
FATHER MUST
HAVE BEEN.

Now arrange the circled letters to form
the surprise answer, as suggested by the
above cartoon.

Print
answer A "◯◯◯◯◯ - ◯◯◯◯◯"
here

JUMBLE®

Unscramble these four Jumbles, one letter to each square, to form four ordinary words.

UNSEE

LAFAT

RANCOB

SURJIT

JOE'S GRILL

CAFE

HE TRIED TO COMPOSE A DRINKING SONG BUT DIDN'T MAKE IT PAST THIS.

Now arrange the circled letters to form the surprise answer, as suggested by the above cartoon.

Print answer here THE ⬡⬡⬡⬡⬡ 2 ⬡⬡⬡⬡

JUMBLE®

Unscramble these four Jumbles, one letter to each square, to form four ordinary words.

ALCKO

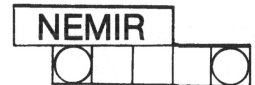

NEMIR

NABACA

CECHIT

THOSE FAMOUS SCULPTURES WERE SURE SOMETHING TO THIS.

Now arrange the circled letters to form the surprise answer, as suggested by the above cartoon.

Print answer here

JUMBLE®

Unscramble these four Jumbles, one letter
to each square, to form four ordinary words.

URRYC

GOBUH

DARIFA

FLUFEM

WHAT YOU MIGHT
SEE IF YOU REFUSE
HER REQUEST FOR
A MINK COAT.

Now arrange the circled letters to form
the surprise answer, as suggested by the
above cartoon.

Print answer here THE ☐◯◯☐ ☐◯◯☐

JUMBLE®

Unscramble these four Jumbles, one letter to each square, to form four ordinary words.

GOOLI

CASHO

CARGIL

BRANER

Soon we'll run out of room for them

WHAT KIND OF A PLACE WAS THAT RABBIT FARM?

Now arrange the circled letters to form the surprise answer, as suggested by the above cartoon.

Print answer here "☐☐☐☐ – ☐☐☐☐☐☐☐"

JUMBLE®

Unscramble these four Jumbles, one letter
to each square, to form four ordinary words.

WULAF

DEEGH

YELMIT

BELEEF

WHAT'S A CATTLE
RUSTLER?

Now arrange the circled letters to form
the surprise answer, as suggested by the
above cartoon.

Print answer here A

JUMBLE®

Unscramble these four Jumbles, one letter to each square, to form four ordinary words.

ALQUI

EMAHR

THARRE

ERAUSS

WHAT THE BROKEN PHONOGRAPH RECORD MUST HAVE BEEN.

Now arrange the circled letters to form the surprise answer, as suggested by the above cartoon.

Print answer here A

JUMBLE®

Unscramble these four Jumbles, one letter
to each square, to form four ordinary words.

KLABY

MOFUR

CROITE

TAMLED

HE SOLD HIS
PRODUCTS TO THE
PICKLE FACTORY.

Now arrange the circled letters to form
the surprise answer, as suggested by the
above cartoon.

Print
answer
here

THE ⭕⭕⭕⭕⭕⭕ IN THE "⭕⭕⭕⭕"

JUMBLE®

Unscramble these four Jumbles, one letter
to each square, to form four ordinary words.

ABISS

TAFOO

KIRBEC

SLEPEN

TAKE OUT

It's the last word

WHAT A GOOD
TONGUE SANDWICH
SHOULD DO.

Now arrange the circled letters to form
the surprise answer, as suggested by the
above cartoon.

Print answer here

FOR

JUMBLE®

Unscramble these four Jumbles, one letter to each square, to form four ordinary words.

NOWRC

AMDAM

FREBLY

BLIMER

He left out a lot

HIS AUTOBIOGRAPHY SHOWED THAT THE ONLY THING WRONG WITH THE AUTHOR WAS THIS.

Now arrange the circled letters to form the surprise answer, as suggested by the above cartoon.

Print answer here HIS

JUMBLE®

Unscramble these four Jumbles, one letter to each square, to form four ordinary words.

CEKEH

BADIE

NETTAX

UNSADE

Fifi!

I'm pooped

HOW DOGS WHO CHASE CARS SOME-TIMES END UP.

Now arrange the circled letters to form the surprise answer, as suggested by the above cartoon.

Print answer here "◯◯◯◯◯◯◯ - ◯◯"

JUMBLE®

Unscramble these four Jumbles, one letter
to each square, to form four ordinary words.

UTOLC

YADEC

TUEBAY

RIQUMS

WEIGHT LIFTERS
IN RESTAURANTS.

Now arrange the circled letters to form
the surprise answer, as suggested by the
above cartoon.

Print answer here

JUMBLE®

Anniversary

Daily Puzzles

JUMBLE®

Unscramble these four Jumbles, one letter
to each square, to form four ordinary words.

ARROD

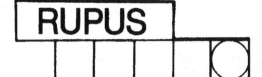

RUPUS

NILUKE

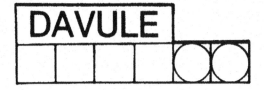

DAVULE

ON A WET DAY,
THIS IS WHERE THEY
HELD A HUDDLE.

Now arrange the circled letters to form
the surprise answer, as suggested by the
above cartoon.

Print answer here   IN A

JUMBLE®

Unscramble these four Jumbles, one letter
to each square, to form four ordinary words.

GEFOB

VURCE

YARAFF

MANNEP

WHAT DO YOU
GET WHEN YOU USE
SOAP AND WATER
ON THE STOVE?

Now arrange the circled letters to form
the surprise answer, as suggested by the
above cartoon.

Print answer here ☐☐☐☐ ON THE ☐☐☐☐☐

JUMBLE®

Unscramble these four Jumbles, one letter
to each square, to form four ordinary words.

KREPY

CAGIM

MODDEO

GEENER

WHAT TO SAY
TO SOMEONE WHO
COMPLAINS OF BEING
A LIGHT SLEEPER.

Now arrange the circled letters to form
the surprise answer, as suggested by the
above cartoon.

*Print answer
here* TRY ⬡⬡⬡⬡⬡ IT IN
THE ⬡⬡⬡⬡

JUMBLE®

Unscramble these four Jumbles, one letter to each square, to form four ordinary words.

OSLOE

VELCO

BLAURT

LOPPIN

THAT CEMETERY WAS UNDER HEAVY SECURITY BECAUSE OF THIS.

Now arrange the circled letters to form the surprise answer, as suggested by the above cartoon.

Print answer here

THE " " THERE

JUMBLE®

Unscramble these four Jumbles, one letter
to each square, to form four ordinary words.

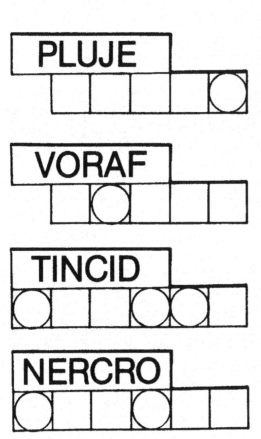

PLUJE

VORAF

TINCID

NERCRO

WHAT GETTING
TO A PICNIC
OFTEN IS NOT.

Now arrange the circled letters to form
the surprise answer, as suggested by the
above cartoon.

Print answer here

JUMBLE®

Unscramble these four Jumbles, one letter
to each square, to form four ordinary words.

WARBL

EMYTH

INTIEF

HAPUNC

Tee
hee

THAT ECCENTRIC
HEN SAT ON
AN AX SO SHE
COULD DO THIS.

Now arrange the circled letters to form
the surprise answer, as suggested by the
above cartoon.

Print answer here " ⬡⬡⬡⬡⬡⬡ – ⬡⬡ "

JUMBLE®

Unscramble these four Jumbles, one letter
to each square, to form four ordinary words.

DRAIC

ELUSO

ALBBUE

OVVEEL

WHAT TOO MUCH
CHAMPAGNE
CAN MAKE A
SINGLE PERSON DO.

Now arrange the circled letters to form
the surprise answer, as suggested by the
above cartoon.

Print answer here

JUMBLE®

Unscramble these four Jumbles, one letter to each square, to form four ordinary words.

UGAVE

THACC

YARTTE

RAWTIE

Beautiful—just beautiful

WHAT THAT GUY WHO WAS ALWAYS LETTING A SMILE BE HIS UMBRELLA ENDED UP WITH.

Now arrange the circled letters to form the surprise answer, as suggested by the above cartoon.

Print answer here

JUMBLE®

Unscramble these four Jumbles, one letter to each square, to form four ordinary words.

TOHOB

DYSUK

CROSCH

FLOBIE

VOTE FOR

He won't budge from his position

WHAT A MAN WHO PLANTS HIS FEET FIRMLY IN THE GROUND SOMETIMES GETS.

Now arrange the circled letters to form the surprise answer, as suggested by the above cartoon.

Print answer here

JUMBLE®

Unscramble these four Jumbles, one letter
to each square, to form four ordinary words.

RODAH

YOPEN

BOILEM

FIDELE

Oh, go ahead

HOW TO GET A GUY
TO DONATE TO
THE BLOOD BANK.

Now arrange the circled letters to form
the surprise answer, as suggested by the
above cartoon.

Print answer here " ⃝⃝⃝⃝⃝⃝ " ⃝⃝⃝

JUMBLE®

Unscramble these four Jumbles, one letter to each square, to form four ordinary words.

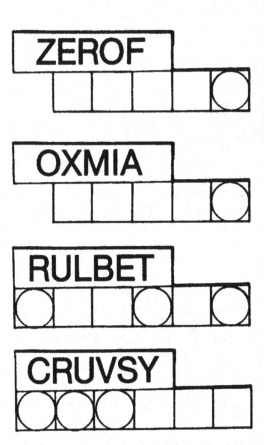

ZEROF

OXMIA

RULBET

CRUVSY

WHAT A MAN WHO TRIES TO ACT LIKE A TOUGH COOKIE OFTEN DOES WHEN PUSH COMES TO SHOVE.

Now arrange the circled letters to form the surprise answer, as suggested by the above cartoon.

Print answer here

JUMBLE®

Unscramble these four Jumbles, one letter to each square, to form four ordinary words.

NALBA

DAAGE

HUNGOE

THALIG

SHE ACCEPTED HIS PROPOSAL BECAUSE HE WAS THIS TYPE OF A GUY.

Now arrange the circled letters to form the surprise answer, as suggested by the above cartoon.

Print answer here AN " ⭕⭕⭕⭕⭕⭕⭕⭕⭕ " ONE

JUMBLE®

Unscramble these four Jumbles, one letter
to each square, to form four ordinary words.

DONEM

CAPIN

FLATUR

LUFUES

WHAT THE
TOW TRUCK WAS
TRYING TO DO
AT THE AUTO RACE.

Now arrange the circled letters to form
the surprise answer, as suggested by the
above cartoon.

*Print
answer
here*

A

JUMBLE®

Unscramble these four Jumbles, one letter
to each square, to form four ordinary words.

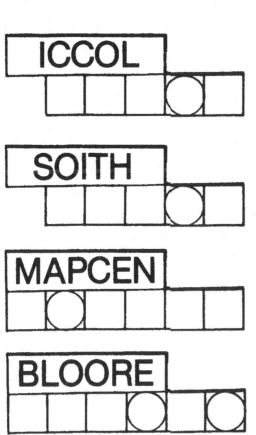

ICCOL

SOITH

MAPCEN

BLOORE

WHAT PIERCES YOUR EAR WITHOUT LEAVING A HOLE?

Now arrange the circled letters to form
the surprise answer, as suggested by the
above cartoon.

Print answer here

JUMBLE ®

Unscramble these four Jumbles, one letter to each square, to form four ordinary words.

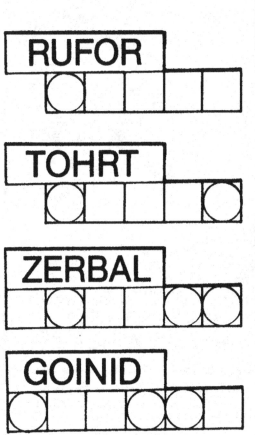

RUFOR

TOHRT

ZERBAL

GOINID

WHAT AN EXCITING
"MATCH" WILL DO
FOR THE FANS.

Now arrange the circled letters to form the surprise answer, as suggested by the above cartoon.

Print answer here  A

JUMBLE®

Unscramble these four Jumbles, one letter to each square, to form four ordinary words.

GINCI

BYMAL

TIGBLE

CEEPIA

HE TOLD THEM HE WAS JUST WHAT THE DOCTOR ORDERED.

Now arrange the circled letters to form the surprise answer, as suggested by the above cartoon.

Print answer here A

JUMBLE®

Unscramble these four Jumbles, one letter to each square, to form four ordinary words.

RAAPK

HANEN

HYRITT

SERJEY

Excuse me, dear

THE MAN WHO MARRIES FOR MONEY WILL USUALLY HAVE TO DO THIS.

Now arrange the circled letters to form the surprise answer, as suggested by the above cartoon.

Print answer here

JUMBLE®

Unscramble these four Jumbles, one letter
to each square, to form four ordinary words.

ZAREC

NOJEY

THRIZE

DOWMIS

Another big gusher!

He sure knows where to find them

WHAT THEY CALLED THAT VERY CLEVER OIL TYCOON.

Now arrange the circled letters to form
the surprise answer, as suggested by the
above cartoon.

Print answer here

THE ◯◯◯◯◯◯ OF "◯◯◯◯"

JUMBLE®

Unscramble these four Jumbles, one letter to each square, to form four ordinary words.

GUNEB

YOHNP

MASHNO

RACCIT

SOME MEN MAKE MONEY WITHOUT WORKING FOR IT FROM SUCKERS WHO WANT TO DO THIS.

STOCKS

Now arrange the circled letters to form the surprise answer, as suggested by the above cartoon.

Print answer here THE ⬡⬡⬡⬡⬡ ⬡⬡⬡⬡⬡⬡

JUMBLE®

Unscramble these four Jumbles, one letter to each square, to form four ordinary words.

ALVIA

YARRT

MOBERY

TOATER

HOW CROSS-EXAM-INATION IS SOME-TIMES CONDUCTED.

Now arrange the circled letters to form the surprise answer, as suggested by the above cartoon.

Print answer here BY ⬡⬡⬡⬡⬡ & ⬡⬡⬡⬡⬡⬡

JUMBLE®

Unscramble these four Jumbles, one letter to each square, to form four ordinary words.

BYLUR

GOLIO

BOUTES

SUNDAI

Hello, Dad . . .

SOME KIDS WHO ARE TALL ENOUGH TO DRIVE THE FAMILY CAR ARE TOO SHORT TO DO THIS.

Now arrange the circled letters to form the surprise answer, as suggested by the above cartoon.

Print answer here ☐☐☐ THE ☐☐☐

JUMBLE®

Unscramble these four Jumbles, one letter
to each square, to form four ordinary words.

MYDOL

MOROG

THACAT

WAYELE

It's the same
all over the
world

WHAT AIR
POLLUTION IS.

Now arrange the circled letters to form
the surprise answer, as suggested by the
above cartoon.

Print
answer NO
here

JUMBLE®

Unscramble these four Jumbles, one letter to each square, to form four ordinary words.

Twenty unexpected guests arriving any minute

INSTANT MEALS

WHEN DINNERS ARE QUICKLY THOUGHT OUT THESE DAYS, THEY'RE OFTEN THIS.

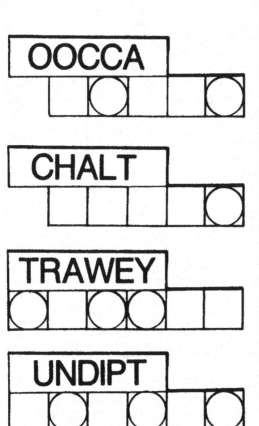

OOCCA

CHALT

TRAWEY

UNDIPT

Now arrange the circled letters to form the surprise answer, as suggested by the above cartoon.

Print answer here

JUMBLE®

Unscramble these four Jumbles, one letter to each square, to form four ordinary words.

ANSPY

ROPAN

TIBESC

HANEEV

Now I'm really hungry

ANOTHER
NAME FOR
"HORS D'OEUVRES."

Now arrange the circled letters to form the surprise answer, as suggested by the above cartoon.

Print answer here

" ⬡⬡⬡⬡ - ⬡⬡⬡⬡⬡⬡⬡ "

JUMBLE®

Unscramble these four Jumbles, one letter
to each square, to form four ordinary words.

ZENOO

RUILD

GROFER

POLEEP

It's chilly
in here

WHAT CAVE ART
MIGHT BE A
PRIMITIVE
FORM OF.

Now arrange the circled letters to form
the surprise answer, as suggested by the
above cartoon.

**Print answer
here** ⬜⬜⬜⬜ " ⬜⬜⬜⬜⬜⬜ "

JUMBLE®

Unscramble these four Jumbles, one letter
to each square, to form four ordinary words.

VAGRE

YAASS

DRALIA

NOYCOT

MANY AFTER-
DINNER SPEAKERS
ARE INCLINED
TO GIVE YOU
MORE THAN THIS.

Now arrange the circled letters to form
the surprise answer, as suggested by the
above cartoon.

Print answer
here   YOU ☐☐☐ ☐☐☐☐☐☐

JUMBLE®

Unscramble these four Jumbles, one letter
to each square, to form four ordinary words.

MEVON

ECKER

HELGGA

AIRFUN

THERE ARE SOME
WOMEN WHO DON'T
OBJECT TO MEN WHO
"LOVE 'EM AND LEAVE
'EM" — PROVIDING
THE MEN DO THIS.

Now arrange the circled letters to form
the surprise answer, as suggested by the
above cartoon.

Print
answer
here

'EM

JUMBLE®

Unscramble these four Jumbles, one letter
to each square, to form four ordinary words.

MUBOX

TUNOF

DOUSTI

RAWDIN

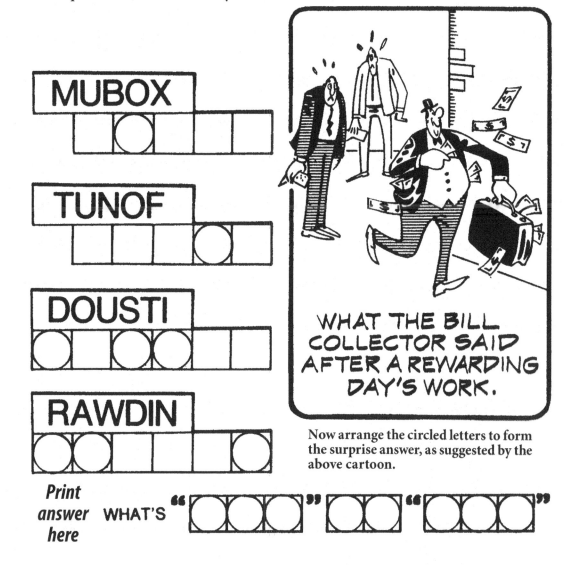

WHAT THE BILL
COLLECTOR SAID
AFTER A REWARDING
DAY'S WORK.

Now arrange the circled letters to form
the surprise answer, as suggested by the
above cartoon.

*Print
answer
here*   WHAT'S " ☐☐☐ " ☐☐ " ☐☐☐ "

JUMBLE®

Unscramble these four Jumbles, one letter
to each square, to form four ordinary words.

OPSOW

SNOBI

LENOTS

SAURES

A COLLECTOR
USUALLY HAS AN
OBSESSION
WITH THIS.

Now arrange the circled letters to form
the surprise answer, as suggested by the
above cartoon.

*Print answer
here*

JUMBLE®

Unscramble these four Jumbles, one letter
to each square, to form four ordinary words.

LYBUL

TELAH

ROWMAR

SAWURL

Move it! How can I beat
the competition?!

HOW THE
SAUSAGE MANU-
FACTURER WANTED
TO MAKE MONEY.

Now arrange the circled letters to form
the surprise answer, as suggested by the
above cartoon.

Print answer here   IN   "◯◯◯◯◯◯" ◯◯◯
THE

JUMBLE®

Unscramble these four Jumbles, one letter to each square, to form four ordinary words.

VOPER

RODLE

SHAUTI

DEECES

He sure gets results

WHAT A GOOD SALESMAN KNOWS HOW TO BRING.

Now arrange the circled letters to form the surprise answer, as suggested by the above cartoon.

Print answer here ⬚⬚⬚⬚⬚⬚⬚ OUT OF ⬚⬚⬚⬚⬚

JUMBLE®

Unscramble these four Jumbles, one letter
to each square, to form four ordinary words.

WORBE

KALNF

CAMBLE

AINNIZ

WHERE THERE'S A
WILL THERE'S
SOMETIMES THIS.

Now arrange the circled letters to form
the surprise answer, as suggested by the
above cartoon.

Print answer here

JUMBLE®

Unscramble these four Jumbles, one letter to each square, to form four ordinary words.

MIRGY

NAHCT

WOLTAL

VEWERS

Sorry I won't be able to make our anniversary party, dear

PEOPLE WHO ARE TOO ANXIOUS TO MAKE A LIVING HAVE SOMETIMES FORGOTTEN THIS.

Now arrange the circled letters to form the surprise answer, as suggested by the above cartoon.

Print answer here ☐☐☐ TO ☐☐☐☐

JUMBLE®

Unscramble these four Jumbles, one letter to each square, to form four ordinary words.

CANEP
◯◯◯◯◯

PLIMB
◯◯◯◯

ONBEAM
◯◯◯◯◯

VINOSI
◯◯◯◯◯

THE JOGGER VISITED THE VETERINARIAN BECAUSE OF THIS.

Now arrange the circled letters to form the surprise answer, as suggested by the above cartoon.

Print answer here   HIS " ◯◯◯◯◯◯ " WERE IN ◯◯◯◯

JUMBLE®

Unscramble these four Jumbles, one letter
to each square, to form four ordinary words.

MYTIA

DENUC

CULIES

RUMMRU

WHAT THE
ORGAN GRINDER
HAD.

Now arrange the circled letters to form
the surprise answer, as suggested by the
above cartoon.

Print answer here A " ⟨⟩⟨⟩⟨⟩⟨⟩ " FOR ⟨⟩⟨⟩⟨⟩⟨⟩⟨⟩

JUMBLE®

Unscramble these four Jumbles, one letter to each square, to form four ordinary words.

CREMY

HEOSU

BTHOLC

HLIFTY

IF HER HUSBAND DIDN'T BUCKLE UP WHILE DRIVING, SHE WAS GOING TO ----

Now arrange the circled letters to form the surprise answer, as suggested by the above cartoon.

Print answer here

JUMBLE®

Unscramble these four Jumbles, one letter
to each square, to form four ordinary words.

VAREB

GREEM

LOSIRA

LAWNTU

He's getting so big!

They get
ugly so
fast.

Can I go
swimming?

THE MONSTERS' TODDLER
WOULDN'T BE HIDEOUS
ENOUGH TO SCARE PEOPLE
UNTIL HE ----

Now arrange the circled letters to form
the surprise answer, as suggested by the
above cartoon.

Print answer here

JUMBLE®

Unscramble these four Jumbles, one letter
to each square, to form four ordinary words.

FINKE

NILTG

TALETT

PHORYT

I can't believe you used to wear those.

It was hard work, but something I had to do.

HIS DIET AND EXERCISE
PROGRAM SUCCEEDED. HE
LOST WEIGHT BECAUSE HE
DIDN'T ----

Now arrange the circled letters to form
the surprise answer, as suggested by the
above cartoon.

Print answer here

JUMBLE®

Unscramble these four Jumbles, one letter
to each square, to form four ordinary words.

LAMTE

SAIBS

CNURHB

LAPOWL

I need you
to point up
more, like
you really
need a ride.

Like this?

THE FASHION SHOOT
FEATURED A MODEL
DRESSED AS A HITCHHIKER
WITH ---

Now arrange the circled letters to form
the surprise answer, as suggested by the
above cartoon.

*Print
answer
here*

" ☐ - ☐☐☐☐☐☐ " ☐☐☐☐☐

JUMBLE®

Unscramble these four Jumbles, one letter
to each square, to form four ordinary words.

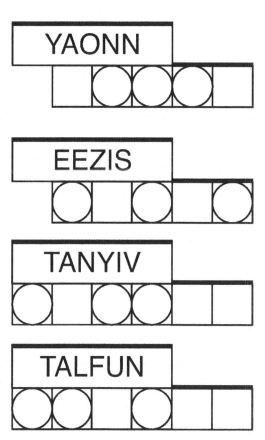

YAONN

EEZIS

TANYIV

TALFUN

Don't take
your eyes
off it.

Our cameras
will capture
it all.

STORM CHASERS WHO ARE
TOO INTENT ON GETTING
CLOSE TO A TWISTER
HAVE ---

Now arrange the circled letters to form
the surprise answer, as suggested by the
above cartoon.

*Print
answer
here*

JUMBLE®

Unscramble these four Jumbles, one letter to each square, to form four ordinary words.

VAYEH

EAEST

MAILAP

VOONYC

I run three marathons a year. I also coach track.

Wow! You're studying podiatry! I can't imagine not hiring you.

HE WOULD BE HIRED AS THEIR NEW SNEAKERS SALESMAN BECAUSE HE WAS A ----

Now arrange the circled letters to form the surprise answer, as suggested by the above cartoon.

Print answer here " ◯◯◯◯◯ " - ◯◯

JUMBLE®

Unscramble these four Jumbles, one letter
to each square, to form four ordinary words.

VAROB

SCUMI

KEDOWR

ATEPUB

I had a 4.
How about
you?

Me, too!
We sure
are getting
around
quickly.

WHEN THEY ADDED UP
THEIR STROKES ON THE
GOLF HOLE, THEY
WERE A ---

Now arrange the circled letters to form
the surprise answer, as suggested by the
above cartoon.

Print answer here " ◯◯◯ - ◯◯◯◯ "

JUMBLE.

Unscramble these four Jumbles, one letter
to each square, to form four ordinary words.

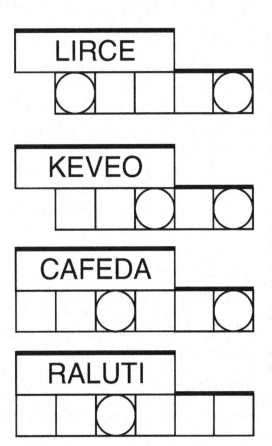

LIRCE

KEVEO

CAFEDA

RALUTI

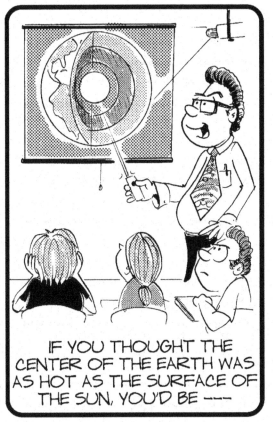

IF YOU THOUGHT THE
CENTER OF THE EARTH WAS
AS HOT AS THE SURFACE OF
THE SUN, YOU'D BE ----

Now arrange the circled letters to form
the surprise answer, as suggested by the
above cartoon.

Print answer here "  "

JUMBLE®

Unscramble these four Jumbles, one letter to each square, to form four ordinary words.

NUBYN

DNAAP

GOTUDU

REMDIA

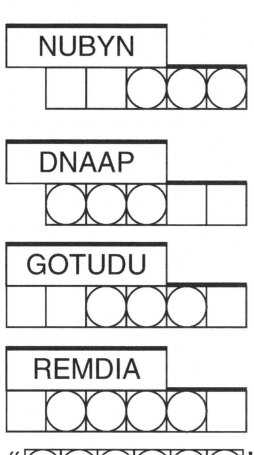

We tried teaching Daisy to speak, but she kept muttering.

Sounds ruff. We tried to teach our dogs to drive, but they couldn't parallel bark.

WITH THE WEEKEND OVER, THE JUMBLE CREATORS STARTED WORKING ON ----

Now arrange the circled letters to form the surprise answer, as suggested by the above cartoon.

Print answer here

" ◯◯◯◯◯◯ "   ◯◯◯◯◯◯◯

JUMBLE®

Unscramble these four Jumbles, one letter to each square, to form four ordinary words.

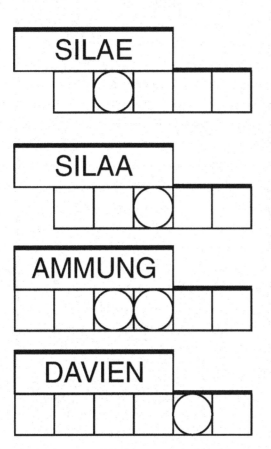

SILAE

SILAA

AMMUNG

DAVIEN

IT WAS DINNERTIME AFTER A LONG DAY OF PLANTING BUSHES AND HE WAS READY TO ---

Now arrange the circled letters to form the surprise answer, as suggested by the above cartoon.

Print answer here

JUMBLE®

Unscramble these four Jumbles, one letter
to each square, to form four ordinary words.

LUDTA

USORC

DAGAPO

NILMYA

HE DIDN'T BUY THE ABACUS
BECAUSE HE WANTED ONE
WITHOUT ---

Now arrange the circled letters to form
the surprise answer, as suggested by the
above cartoon.

Print answer here ⬭⬭⬭ - ⬭⬭⬭

JUMBLE®

Unscramble these four Jumbles, one letter to each square, to form four ordinary words.

NHITN

YIRAN

YARVOS

ERNTUU

WHEN IT CAME TO THOMAS EDISON'S INNOVATIONS, THE MUSEUM HAD AN IMPRESSIVE ----

Now arrange the circled letters to form the surprise answer, as suggested by the above cartoon.

Print answer here ⬡⬡⬡⬡⬡⬡ - ⬡⬡⬡

JUMBLE®

Unscramble these four Jumbles, one letter to each square, to form four ordinary words.

SNUTT

TEYLS

UUEQIN

KEERAB

Did you get a cash advance on your credit card when you were in Vegas? You're paying 25% on that.

GETTING A CASH ADVANCE ON HIS CREDIT CARD WASN'T IN HIS ----

Now arrange the circled letters to form the surprise answer, as suggested by the above cartoon.

Print answer here

JUMBLE®

Unscramble these four Jumbles, one letter to each square, to form four ordinary words.

RILTF

ODSUE

FURFNO

TREETH

Available $1,000 per month

Available $1,500 per month

Is that one worth $500.00 more a month?

No. They are identical.

BOTH HOUSES WERE FOR LEASE, AND THEIR DECISION WOULD BE BASED ON THE ---

Now arrange the circled letters to form the surprise answer, as suggested by the above cartoon.

Print answer here " ⬡⬡⬡⬡⬡⬡ - ⬡⬡⬡⬡⬡ "

JUMBLE®

Unscramble these four Jumbles, one letter
to each square, to form four ordinary words.

PNETS

SENYO

NPARIS

URBBSU

When David gives me a
bonus answer I don't
get, I draw blank faces.

Yes. Good
Jumbles mix
him up.

JUMBLE LIVE!

Aren't they
clever.

What great
jobs they
have.

WHEN THE JUMBLE
CREATORS APPEARED AT
THE LIVE EVENT, EVERYONE
ENJOYED THEIR ----

Now arrange the circled letters to form
the surprise answer, as suggested by the
above cartoon.

Print
answer
here

"⬡⬡⬡⬡⬡" ⬡⬡⬡⬡⬡⬡⬡⬡⬡

JUMBLE®

Unscramble these four Jumbles, one letter to each square, to form four ordinary words.

TIKYT

CUJIE

VIRUQE

OPMMPO

Is your husband still working on that doghouse?

He works on it all the time.

BUILDING AN ELABORATE DOGHOUSE IN THE BACKYARD WAS HIS ----

Now arrange the circled letters to form the surprise answer, as suggested by the above cartoon.

Print answer here

JUMBLE®

Unscramble these four Jumbles, one letter
to each square, to form four ordinary words.

KENAL

CONTH

BBROSA

SQUIBE

Look. It's our lucky day.

Happy March 17th!

Have you been good?

Someone needs to check his calendar.

IF CHRISTMAS WAS
HELD ON MARCH 17, THEN
WE'D GET ----

Now arrange the circled letters to form
the surprise answer, as suggested by the
above cartoon.

*Print
answer
here*

" ☐☐☐☐☐ - ☐ ' - ☐☐☐☐☐ "

JUMBLE®

Unscramble these four Jumbles, one letter to each square, to form four ordinary words.

DUYAG

CAAKB

CALUTA

LABOLT

We have enough orders to keep us busy for weeks.

We actually have too many orders for what we have on hand.

THE FIREWOOD BUSINESS WAS DOING SO WELL THAT THERE WAS A ———

Now arrange the circled letters to form the surprise answer, as suggested by the above cartoon.

Print answer here

JUMBLE.

Unscramble these four Jumbles, one letter
to each square, to form four ordinary words.

REAWF

MURYM

OPSYKO

NOFYLD

Wow!
That's like
magic.

The ink is permanent!

THIS WILL BE

THE INVENTOR OF THE
FELT TIP PEN SAID, "THESE
WILL BE A BIG HIT, ‒‒‒"

Now arrange the circled letters to form
the surprise answer, as suggested by the
above cartoon.

*Print
answer
here*

JUMBLE®

Unscramble these four Jumbles, one letter
to each square, to form four ordinary words.

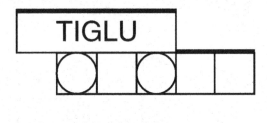

TIGLU

NETVE

REVGNO

DIRBOF

As your king,
I declare today a
day of rejoicing.

What a
glorious
day for a
coronation.

'Tis a
good
sign!

THERE WASN'T A CLOUD IN
THE SKY WHEN THE NEW
KING BEGAN ----

Now arrange the circled letters to form
the surprise answer, as suggested by the
above cartoon.

Print answer here

JUMBLE®

Unscramble these four Jumbles, one letter to each square, to form four ordinary words.

KEIRH

ATOLG

RAFSIA

BOMOAB

$600 for the tires. Plus the tow fee.

I don't have any cash. This will max out the card.

AFTER CARELESSLY PUNCTURING ALL FOUR TIRES, HE WOULD BE ----

Now arrange the circled letters to form the surprise answer, as suggested by the above cartoon.

Print answer here

JUMBLE®

Unscramble these four Jumbles, one letter to each square, to form four ordinary words.

CADYE

NOOZE

RIXEPE

PARSIN

Fields are tilled. Check. Tractor gassed up. Check. Bins full. Check. We're ready to go.

What's next?

IT WAS TIME TO PLANT THE CORN, AND THE FARMER WAS READY TO ---

Now arrange the circled letters to form the surprise answer, as suggested by the above cartoon.

Print answer here "◯◯◯-◯◯◯◯"

JUMBLE®

Unscramble these four Jumbles, one letter
to each square, to form four ordinary words.

CREHP

RUMLE

AMAREC

TANBOY

APSIS CO.

I've seen enough.

I'll start an investigation

These numbers don't add up.

AFTER DISCOVERING FRAUD
AT THE AEROSPACE
COMPANY, THEY WOULD
NEED TO ----

Now arrange the circled letters to form
the surprise answer, as suggested by the
above cartoon.

Print
answer
here

JUMBLE®

Unscramble these four Jumbles, one letter to each square, to form four ordinary words.

TORBO

GILCO

WEALYE

REMMEB

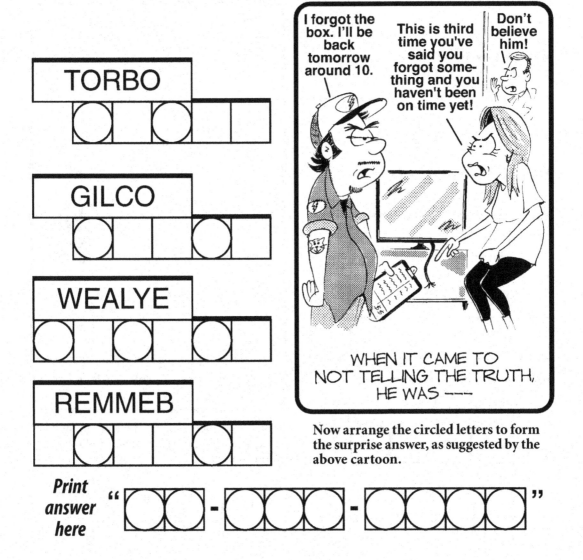

I forgot the box. I'll be back tomorrow around 10.

This is third time you've said you forgot something and you haven't been on time yet!

Don't believe him!

WHEN IT CAME TO NOT TELLING THE TRUTH, HE WAS ----

Now arrange the circled letters to form the surprise answer, as suggested by the above cartoon.

Print answer here

" ☐☐ - ☐☐☐ - ☐☐☐☐ "

JUMBLE®

Unscramble these four Jumbles, one letter to each square, to form four ordinary words.

LABFE

ETNTE

DIROHA

SIPOME

Wow! I'm glad we spent the extra money on this one.

It was the best one they had.

THEIR KITE FLEW SO WELL BECAUSE IT WAS ----

Now arrange the circled letters to form the surprise answer, as suggested by the above cartoon.

Print answer here

◯◯◯ - ◯◯ - ◯◯◯ - ◯◯◯◯

JUMBLE®

Unscramble these four Jumbles, one letter to each square, to form four ordinary words.

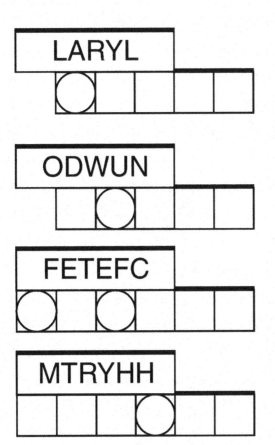

LARYL

ODWUN

FETEFC

MTRYHH

You really know how to design them.

It's what I do best.

HE SPECIALIZED IN BUILDING SECURE STRUCTURES FOR TROOPS. IT WAS HIS ---

Now arrange the circled letters to form the surprise answer, as suggested by the above cartoon.

Print answer here

JUMBLE®

Unscramble these four Jumbles, one letter to each square, to form four ordinary words.

PUSOY

RESIK

POLTEP

MUVUCA

There are billions of stars in the Milky Way. And to think, our closest neighbor is 2.5 million light years away.

THE UNIVERSE IS HOME TO SO MANY PLANETS, STARS AND GALAXIES BECAUSE IT'S ---

Now arrange the circled letters to form the surprise answer, as suggested by the above cartoon.

Print answer here

JUMBLE®

Unscramble these four Jumbles, one letter to each square, to form four ordinary words.

RUMON

SIHTO

SWERDH

CURPES

Why so down?

You're not funny!

HIS RIVAL AT THE HOT AIR BALLOON RACE ----

Now arrange the circled letters to form the surprise answer, as suggested by the above cartoon.

Print answer here

JUMBLE ®

Unscramble these four Jumbles, one letter
to each square, to form four ordinary words.

UDELE

LEYID

SEEGRY

NUBODA

People would come from miles
around to taste her milk.
Her cheese won 12 straight blue
ribbons.

So, it's
true?

HE TOLD STORIES ABOUT
THE COW THAT HAD
PRODUCED SO MUCH MILK
BECAUSE SHE WAS ----

Now arrange the circled letters to form
the surprise answer, as suggested by the
above cartoon.

*Print
answer
here*

" ◯◯◯◯◯◯ - ◯◯◯◯◯ "

JUMBLE®

Unscramble these four Jumbles, one letter
to each square, to form four ordinary words.

MURYM

RAHDO

SINGUE

LAIHEN

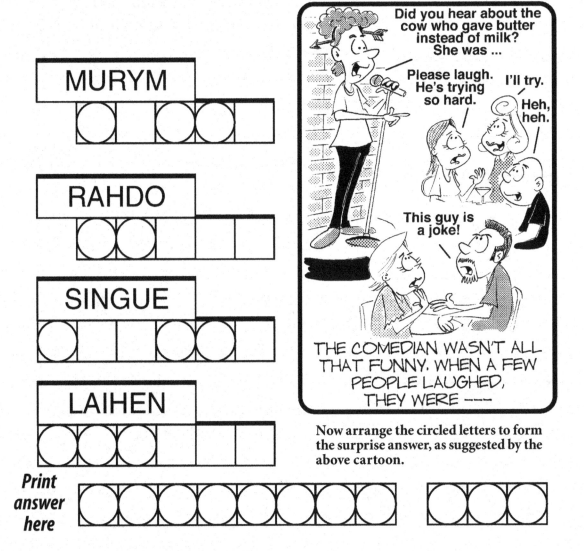

Did you hear about the
cow who gave butter
instead of milk?
She was ...

Please laugh.
He's trying
so hard.

I'll try.

Heh,
heh.

This guy is
a joke!

THE COMEDIAN WASN'T ALL
THAT FUNNY. WHEN A FEW
PEOPLE LAUGHED,
THEY WERE ----

Now arrange the circled letters to form
the surprise answer, as suggested by the
above cartoon.

*Print
answer
here*

JUMBLE®

Unscramble these four Jumbles, one letter to each square, to form four ordinary words.

GREEV

CATHH

CLENGA

DARUSB

Here. You need to hold your fingers like this.

Thanks for the help.

SHE WAS STRUGGLING TO LEARN SIGN LANGUAGE, SO THE INSTRUCTOR ----

Now arrange the circled letters to form the surprise answer, as suggested by the above cartoon.

Print answer here

JUMBLE®

Unscramble these four Jumbles, one letter
to each square, to form four ordinary words.

ZEOON

TRIDY

HECONS

CEDIET

How 'bout I meet you at
the room after I play a
little craps?

You're
kidding me,
right?

C'mon, 10 the
hard way!

HE ASKED HIS WIFE IF HE
COULD PLAY CRAPS, BUT
SHE SAID ---

Now arrange the circled letters to form
the surprise answer, as suggested by the
above cartoon.

Print answer here

JUMBLE®

Unscramble these four Jumbles, one letter to each square, to form four ordinary words.

SKAHY

PROMH

AGUTEO

BBOLEB

We're having a big 60th birthday party for me.

The grandkids love fireworks. I'm only 59, by the way.

Would you like earplugs with that?

THE CUSTOMERS AT THE FIREWORKS STORE WERE ---

Now arrange the circled letters to form the surprise answer, as suggested by the above cartoon.

Print answer here

JUMBLE®

Unscramble these four Jumbles, one letter to each square, to form four ordinary words.

AGREW

DUYMD

RUSASE

NOCUBE

It can help you add any numbers together.

This is the greatest thing I've ever seen!

WHEN HE SHOWED HIS WIFE THE ABACUS HE'D BOUGHT, SHE THOUGHT IT WAS ---

Now arrange the circled letters to form the surprise answer, as suggested by the above cartoon.

Print answer here " ☐☐☐ - ☐☐☐ "

JUMBLE®

Unscramble these four Jumbles, one letter to each square, to form four ordinary words.

SONOW

PRUNS

DEODOL

ANUIGA

You must be climbing all the time.

Not all the time. It comes and goes with the weather.

HE WAS EXPLAINING TO THE CLIMBER THAT BEING A SHERPA HAD ITS ----

Now arrange the circled letters to form the surprise answer, as suggested by the above cartoon.

Print answer here

JUMBLE®

Unscramble these four Jumbles, one letter
to each square, to form four ordinary words.

NYEPN

BOMMA

MISWHY

FEDDIE

HE COULDN'T REMEMBER
WHAT TIME THE SUN WOULD
RISE, BUT THEN IT ---

Now arrange the circled letters to form
the surprise answer, as suggested by the
above cartoon.

Print
answer
here

JUMBLE®

Unscramble these four Jumbles, one letter to each square, to form four ordinary words.

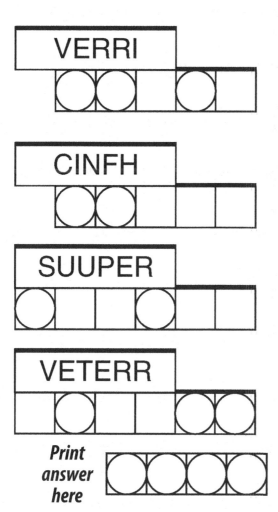

VERRI

CINFH

SUUPER

VETERR

Print answer here

Now listen. We do things a certain way. Now start booing!

Go ahead and boo. I'm going to mess with the tv!

He just does what he wants!

ONE GHOST DIDN'T FIT IN WITH THE REST BECAUSE HE WAS A ---

Now arrange the circled letters to form the surprise answer, as suggested by the above cartoon.

JUMBLE®

Unscramble these four Jumbles, one letter to each square, to form four ordinary words.

SYNAP

HNIYS

TTREEW

DOGAPA

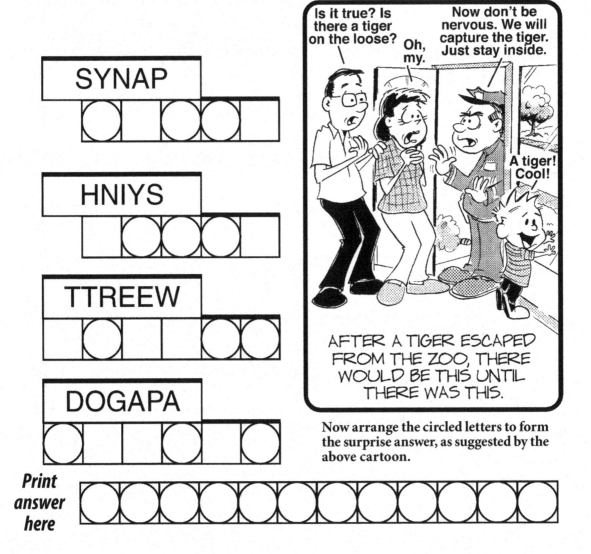

Is it true? Is there a tiger on the loose?

Oh, my.

Now don't be nervous. We will capture the tiger. Just stay inside.

A tiger! Cool!

AFTER A TIGER ESCAPED FROM THE ZOO, THERE WOULD BE THIS UNTIL THERE WAS THIS.

Now arrange the circled letters to form the surprise answer, as suggested by the above cartoon.

Print answer here

JUMBLE®

Unscramble these four Jumbles, one letter
to each square, to form four ordinary words.

ATING

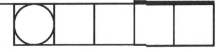
PIMLE

DERTON

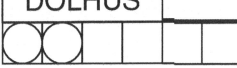
DOLHUS

I thought we were going to be planting, not partying.

C'mon, let's twist!

Turn it up!

WHEN NEIGHBORS HELPED THEM INSTALL THEIR NEW LANDSCAPING, THEY HAD A ----

Now arrange the circled letters to form the surprise answer, as suggested by the above cartoon.

Print answer here

JUMBLE®

Unscramble these four Jumbles, one letter to each square, to form four ordinary words.

MUBLP

RALUR

NECTAC

TUNBOY

It's a great size for going place to place.

Our bedroom is on the left.

THEY COULD SAIL THEIR NEW BOAT FROM KEY WEST TO MIAMI TO BOSTON BECAUSE IT WAS ---

Now arrange the circled letters to form the surprise answer, as suggested by the above cartoon.

Print answer here ◯◯◯◯ - ◯◯◯◯

102

JUMBLE®

Unscramble these four Jumbles, one letter to each square, to form four ordinary words.

TECOT

MURST

MERHOC

KAWYLE

What makes her so special?

I can sell her milk at twice the price of the others.

ELSIE

THE DAIRY FARMER WAS MAKING HUGE PROFITS. HE LOVED HIS ---

Now arrange the circled letters to form the surprise answer, as suggested by the above cartoon.

Print answer here

JUMBLE®

Unscramble these four Jumbles, one letter
to each square, to form four ordinary words.

FRIEG

FINEK

AGLONO

POLTPA

You have to swear
you'll keep this
between us.

Oh, my.

WHEN IT CAME TO WHETHER
OR NOT SHE'D BE ABLE TO
KEEP A SECRET,
THERE WAS ----

Now arrange the circled letters to form
the surprise answer, as suggested by the
above cartoon.

Print answer
here

JUMBLE®

Unscramble these four Jumbles, one letter to each square, to form four ordinary words.

CUNED

LATYL

VORYOG

RORISE

It goes round and round the foot stick.

Wow! I'll give you my fire stone for one.

THE INVENTION OF THE WHEEL WAS ---

Now arrange the circled letters to form the surprise answer, as suggested by the above cartoon.

Print answer here

JUMBLE®

Unscramble these four Jumbles, one letter
to each square, to form four ordinary words.

VICLI

GINIC

NOPELL

LURPEY

How's it going? It's a
little different than
elementary school,
I imagine.

Principal
Jackson to
the office,
now! Please!

I should never
have taken
this job.

BEING THE PRINCIPAL OF A
HIGH SCHOOL HAD SEEMED
LIKE SUCH A GOOD IDEA, ----

Now arrange the circled letters to form
the surprise answer, as suggested by the
above cartoon.

*Print
answer
here*

JUMBLE®

Unscramble these four Jumbles, one letter to each square, to form four ordinary words.

EVGIN

SENHE

BIHDEN

SAMHAT

What's with all the bushes?

Your turn, Bob.

I'm going all in with privacy.

HE HAD BUSHES TO BLOCK OUT HIS NEIGHBORS, BUT HE PLANTED SOME MORE TO ----

Now arrange the circled letters to form the surprise answer, as suggested by the above cartoon.

Print answer here

JUMBLE®

Unscramble these four Jumbles, one letter
to each square, to form four ordinary words.

WETIN

NORYI

WRIYEN

SIVETN

The waiter
is going to
slip on the
puddle.

The glasses
of wine will
spill on the
woman.

Whoa! How did
you boys know
that?

THE TWINS HAD INCREDIBLE
POWERS OF PERCEPTION.
THEY WERE VERY ----

Now arrange the circled letters to form
the surprise answer, as suggested by the
above cartoon.

*Print
answer
here* " ◯◯ - ◯◯◯ - ◯◯◯◯◯ "

JUMBLE®

Unscramble these four Jumbles, one letter to each square, to form four ordinary words.

GROOF

KUYHS

GNHELT

CANGLE

Oh, no! That wasn't the way it was supposed to fall!

What were you thinking?

HE'D PLANNED TO CUT THE TREE DOWN WITHOUT ANY PROBLEMS, BUT HIS PLANS ---

Now arrange the circled letters to form the surprise answer, as suggested by the above cartoon.

Print answer here

109

JUMBLE®

Unscramble these four Jumbles, one letter to each square, to form four ordinary words.

SITOH

TAMEL

ELAGIO

BEMLIN

Looks like I'll never fit into my uniform again.

You're going to fight those fried foods and wear that uniform.

THE RETIRED ARMY GENERAL TRIED TO LOSE WEIGHT, BUT IT WAS A ---

Now arrange the circled letters to form the surprise answer, as suggested by the above cartoon.

Print answer here

JUMBLE®

Unscramble these four Jumbles, one letter to each square, to form four ordinary words.

GRETI

FEHTT

OKERIO

LETOTU

How are you doing?

He's just showing off.

What's his deal?

WHEN THE STALLION NOTICED THE ATTRACTIVE MARE IN THE PASTURE, HE WAS ---

Now arrange the circled letters to form the surprise answer, as suggested by the above cartoon.

Print answer here

JUMBLE®

Unscramble these four Jumbles, one letter to each square, to form four ordinary words.

CARTK

FARHW

COENER

TIRECM

He loves this couch.

We can't have him ruin another.

THE SOFA THE DOG SLEPT ON WAS IN ROUGH SHAPE BECAUSE OF ALL THE ----

Now arrange the circled letters to form the surprise answer, as suggested by the above cartoon.

Print answer here

AND " "

JUMBLE®

Unscramble these four Jumbles, one letter
to each square, to form four ordinary words.

PEWST

SIABS

ALATUC

REDVIT

I just
wanted to
sell my
watch!

For only $50? The
one that say's
Happy 50th
Anniversary?

THE UNDERCOVER COP
BOUGHT THE ROLEX FROM
THE STREET VENDOR
BECAUSE ---

Now arrange the circled letters to form
the surprise answer, as suggested by the
above cartoon.

*Print
answer
here*

113

JUMBLE®

Unscramble these four Jumbles, one letter
to each square, to form four ordinary words.

FARCS

CULYK

TATINA

CLIPYO

Cool!
It's
Vulcan
nerve
pinch
time!

What an
amazing skill.

He was the
best!

EVERYONE LOVED LEONARD
NIMOY'S ROLE AS A VULCAN
AND THOUGHT HE WAS ----

Now arrange the circled letters to form
the surprise answer, as suggested by the
above cartoon.

Print
answer
here

"   "

JUMBLE®

Unscramble these four Jumbles, one letter
to each square, to form four ordinary words.

SLAFK

SAREO

DUEXLE

TUTELO

He's resolved to be ready for the Olympics.

Wow! He's so focused on sprinting!

WHEN IT CAME TO TRAINING
FOR RACES, THE SPRINTER
WAS ––––

Now arrange the circled letters to form
the surprise answer, as suggested by the
above cartoon.

Print answer here

JUMBLE®

Unscramble these four Jumbles, one letter to each square, to form four ordinary words.

NUMOD

CARNH

PELSEY

LILWOW

Can you take a break from the Jumble puns to go to the beach?

What are we wading for?

WHEN THE "PUNNY" GUY WAS ASKED IF HE'D LIKE TO GO TO THE BEACH, HE SAID ----

Now arrange the circled letters to form the surprise answer, as suggested by the above cartoon.

Print answer here

" "

JUMBLE®

Unscramble these four Jumbles, one letter to each square, to form four ordinary words.

CRIBH

PODAT

HITREE

BARTBI

We'll have you back in shape in no time.

It certainly has improved.

THE PHYSICAL THERAPIST'S OFFICE WAS A LITTLE RUN-DOWN, SO SHE ----

Now arrange the circled letters to form the surprise answer, as suggested by the above cartoon.

Print answer here

JUMBLE®

Unscramble these four Jumbles, one letter
to each square, to form four ordinary words.

LORTL

WHONS

TOCENA

NEDTOE

So,
which
will it
be?

I think we'll
take the one
with the pond.

I say we
take the
one with
the stream.

THE PIONEERING COUPLE
ARGUED ABOUT WHICH
TRACT OF LAND TO BUILD
ON AND COULDN'T ----

Now arrange the circled letters to form
the surprise answer, as suggested by the
above cartoon.

*Print
answer
here*

JUMBLE®

Unscramble these four Jumbles, one letter to each square, to form four ordinary words.

GALIE
◯◯◯◯

ODORE
◯◯◯◯◯

RETVAN
◯◯◯◯◯◯

NNNACO
◯◯◯◯◯◯

Hello! Thank you...OK. I have already begun to hypnotize some of you! You hear only my voice.

Hypno Harry

Bob! Can you hear me?

THE HYPNOTIST MADE A ---

Now arrange the circled letters to form the surprise answer, as suggested by the above cartoon.

Print answer here

◯◯◯◯◯◯   ◯◯-◯◯◯◯◯◯

JUMBLE®

Unscramble these four Jumbles, one letter to each square, to form four ordinary words.

VEEKO

PAYPL

NASOSE

TEVORL

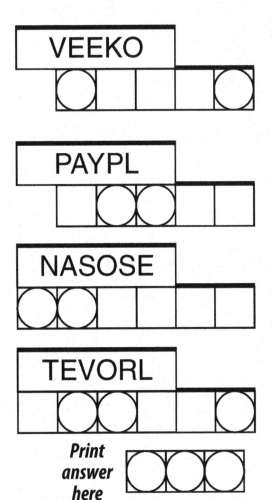

Mr. Scotty will only take bottled water. If it's too warm, he won't drink it. Ms. Poofy only likes to be scratched front to back or she'll claw you. And don't speak too loudly.

HER CAT AND DOG WERE HIGH MAINTENANCE BECAUSE THEY HAD SO MANY ----

Now arrange the circled letters to form the surprise answer, as suggested by the above cartoon.

Print answer here

JUMBLE®

Unscramble these four Jumbles, one letter
to each square, to form four ordinary words.

BADIE

THYEF

BEMMEL

MASLID

It will keep out all rain and drafts. It's proven to reduce heating bills by 60%. And, it's half off. Sold!

WHEN IT CAME TO BUYING
WEATHER STRIPPING, THE
FACT THAT IT WAS
ON SALE ----

Now arrange the circled letters to form
the surprise answer, as suggested by the
above cartoon.

*Print
answer
here*

121

JUMBLE®

Unscramble these four Jumbles, one letter to each square, to form four ordinary words.

BIHAT

KRIHE

ACCELK

TOLBET

We really need to get together soon.

CHEVETTE

Looks like you're going to have company on the way home.

HDNSND1

13.1

THE MOTHER BIRD TRANSPORTED HER EGGS IN A ---

Now arrange the circled letters to form the surprise answer, as suggested by the above cartoon.

Print answer here

122

JUMBLE

Unscramble these four Jumbles, one letter
to each square, to form four ordinary words.

CEYDA

LEPSL

TRRIWE

GNURHY

THE IDENTITY OF
THE MUMMY WAS ---

Now arrange the circled letters to form
the surprise answer, as suggested by the
above cartoon.

*Print
answer
here*

JUMBLE®

Unscramble these four Jumbles, one letter to each square, to form four ordinary words.

PUYOS

HURSE

NIECCS

REDONY

Is anyone angry about the stories you've shared?

John, Sammy, and Sir Paul called. They've canceled their sessions with you.

They'd call me if they were.

CRACK! BOOM! BAM! KENNY ARONOFF

THE DRUMMER'S TELL-ALL AUTOBIOGRAPHY HAD ---

Now arrange the circled letters to form the surprise answer, as suggested by the above cartoon.

Print answer here

JUMBLE®

Unscramble these four Jumbles, one letter to each square, to form four ordinary words.

POMOH

LODIY

SKYCIL

DISBEE

I'd like one ticket, please.

I'm sorry. We are completely sold out.

Authors
Knurek/Hoyt-
JUMBLE
Rowling-
Sherri Potter
Brown-
Jumble Code

THE LIBRARY WAS HAVING A SERIES OF AUTHORS SPEAK AND WAS ----

Now arrange the circled letters to form the surprise answer, as suggested by the above cartoon.

Print answer here

JUMBLE®

Unscramble these four Jumbles, one letter to each square, to form four ordinary words.

PRUUS

POLEE

NYKODE

ATUPIO

I love when you have on a few extra pounds.

You're sweet. I have to go. A cargo ship is coming in.

Arnold Harbor

THE HARBORMASTER WAS A LITTLE OVERWEIGHT, BUT HIS WIFE LIKED HIM ON THE ----

Now arrange the circled letters to form the surprise answer, as suggested by the above cartoon.

Print answer here

JUMBLE®

Unscramble these four Jumbles, one letter to each square, to form four ordinary words.

RAPOE

TIWYT

WOLLYS

GEDDER

I guess I overbought. You kids take what you want.

Wow! What a treat! I'll take three, please.

WHEN SHE STARTED TO GIVE OUT EXTRA CANDY, THE TRICK-OR-TREATERS THOUGHT IT WAS A ---

Now arrange the circled letters to form the surprise answer, as suggested by the above cartoon.

Print answer here

JUMBLE®

Unscramble these four Jumbles, one letter
to each square, to form four ordinary words.

PAHYP

KLUPC

CLATEK

CCITHE

I'm not paying you by the hour. Can you finish before midnight?

Do you have any coffee?

THE MOVERS HAD NO PROBLEMS LIFTING THE HEAVY BOXES, BUT SHE WANTED THEM TO ---

Now arrange the circled letters to form the surprise answer, as suggested by the above cartoon.

Print answer here

128

JUMBLE®

Unscramble these four Jumbles, one letter
to each square, to form four ordinary words.

BIROT

ROWDL

KYLELI

DIQULI

I was just
shooting at
some food,
and up
came this
bubblin'
crude.

We're going
to be rich!
Let's move!

AFTER DISCOVERING OIL ON
THEIR PROPERTY, THEY
WOULD BECOME ---

Now arrange the circled letters to form
the surprise answer, as suggested by the
above cartoon.

Print answer
here

◯◯◯◯ - ◯◯ - ◯◯

JUMBLE®

Unscramble these four Jumbles, one letter to each square, to form four ordinary words.

PENIT

TOAIR

WORNAD

QUAPOE

How did you get Billy King here?

I told him people were going to think he was chicken if he didn't compete. And I paid him a ton.

THE COWBOY DIDN'T WANT TO PARTICIPATE IN THE RODEO, BUT HE GOT ---

Now arrange the circled letters to form the surprise answer, as suggested by the above cartoon.

Print answer here

JUMBLE®

Unscramble these four Jumbles, one letter
to each square, to form four ordinary words.

HOCAV

FERIG

TRARHE

TRIHTS

Wow! Will
you be able
to monitor it
up there?

It has
every bell
and
whistle out
there.
It will work
at any
altitude.

THE FANCY NEW
WEATHER BALLOON
WAS ---

Now arrange the circled letters to form
the surprise answer, as suggested by the
above cartoon.

Print answer here ◯◯◯◯ - ◯◯◯◯

JUMBLE®

Unscramble these four Jumbles, one letter
to each square, to form four ordinary words.

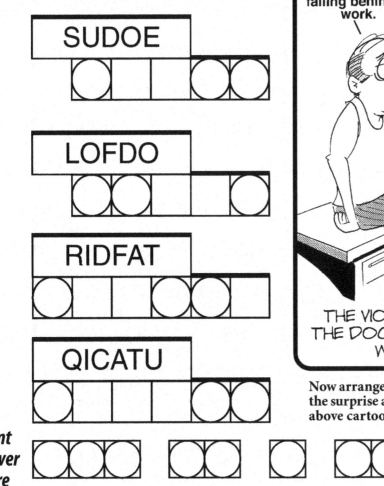

SUDOE

LOFDO

RIDFAT

QICATU

"I just don't have any energy. I keep falling behind at work."

"You need to eat better and exercise. Let's get you into shape."

THE VIOLINIST WENT TO THE DOCTOR BECAUSE HE WASN'T ---

Now arrange the circled letters to form
the surprise answer, as suggested by the
above cartoon.

Print
answer
here

132

JUMBLE®

Unscramble these four Jumbles, one letter
to each square, to form four ordinary words.

ZALEG

DUMYD

PENOLY

MARLCO

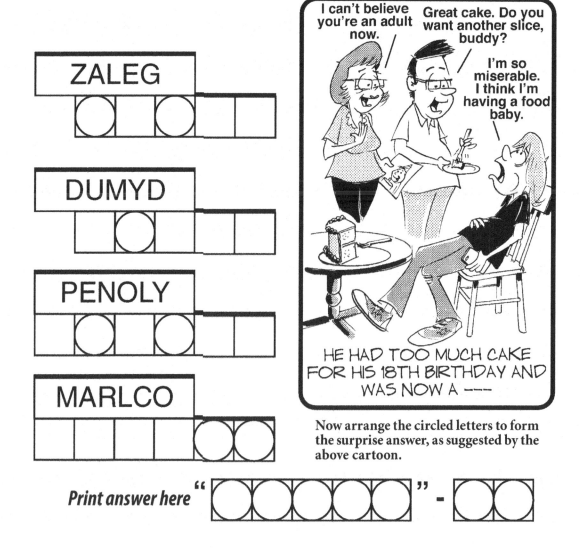

I can't believe you're an adult now.

Great cake. Do you want another slice, buddy?

I'm so miserable. I think I'm having a food baby.

HE HAD TOO MUCH CAKE
FOR HIS 18TH BIRTHDAY AND
WAS NOW A ----

Now arrange the circled letters to form
the surprise answer, as suggested by the
above cartoon.

Print answer here " ◯◯◯◯◯ " - ◯◯

JUMBLE.

Unscramble these four Jumbles, one letter
to each square, to form four ordinary words.

SOKIK

NERDT

DOGRUN

HBRARO

I want to look
my best for
my girl.

The dust in the
tunnel is bad
for your skin.

THE PRISON INMATE USED
ACNE CREAM BECAUSE HE
WAS ---

Now arrange the circled letters to form
the surprise answer, as suggested by the
above cartoon.

*Print
answer
here*

JUMBLE®

Unscramble these four Jumbles, one letter to each square, to form four ordinary words.

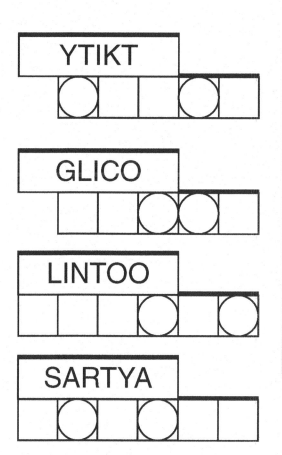

YTIKT

GLICO

LINTOO

SARTYA

His looks are bowling me over.

He has hair to spare.

Keep it up. You're perfect, so far.

THE HANDSOME BOWLER WAS ---

Now arrange the circled letters to form the surprise answer, as suggested by the above cartoon.

Print answer here

JUMBLE®

Unscramble these four Jumbles, one letter
to each square, to form four ordinary words.

SIDYA

SOREA

CDENHR

RACDOC

Dude, how was
your Friday night?
Are you crying?

Kathy broke up
with me last night.

WHEN HIS GIRLFRIEND
BROKE UP WITH HIM ON
FRIDAY, THE WEEKEND
STARTED ON A ----

Now arrange the circled letters to form
the surprise answer, as suggested by the
above cartoon.

Print answer " ◯◯◯◯◯◯ - ◯◯◯ "
here

136

JUMBLE®

Unscramble these four Jumbles, one letter to each square, to form four ordinary words.

FINKE

KAWET

SERDYS

RVAYIA

I think we're good here. Let's call it a night.

Yep. I'm heading out.

MICK AND KEITH WORKED ON "(I CAN'T GET NO) SATISFACTION" UNTIL THEY ----

Now arrange the circled letters to form the surprise answer, as suggested by the above cartoon.

Print answer here

JUMBLE®

Unscramble these four Jumbles, one letter to each square, to form four ordinary words.

MOSTP

LEERD

PACTEC

DARIHO

Wasn't this supposed to be your shoot?

I invented that look! She's got to go.

THE FASHION MODEL DIDN'T LIKE HER NEW COMPETITION AND THOUGHT SHE ----

Now arrange the circled letters to form the surprise answer, as suggested by the above cartoon.

Print answer here

JUMBLE®

Unscramble these four Jumbles, one letter
to each square, to form four ordinary words.

MFIYL

NALGC

SAFCIO

NARPIS

When did you
know that you
wanted to be
a quarterback?

I've always
known.

HE PLAYED QB IN HIGH
SCHOOL, COLLEGE AND
NOW THE NFL BECAUSE
BEING A QB WASN'T A ----

Now arrange the circled letters to form
the surprise answer, as suggested by the
above cartoon.

Print
answer
here

JUMBLE®

Unscramble these four Jumbles, one letter
to each square, to form four ordinary words.

NERTD

GIRDN

HAYMME

SECASC

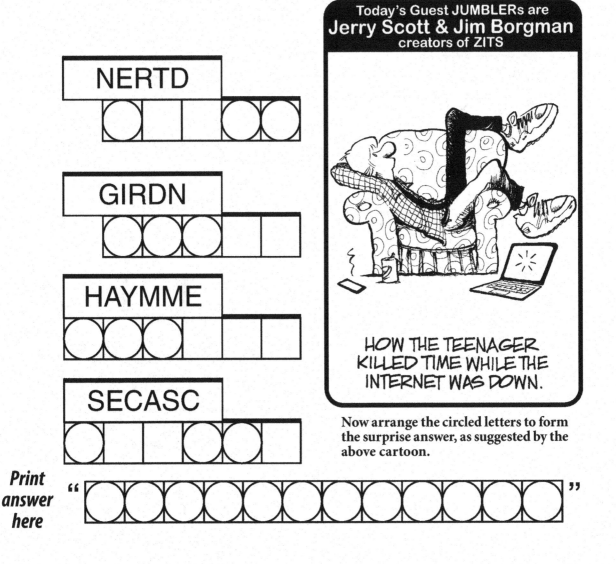

Today's Guest JUMBLERs are
Jerry Scott & Jim Borgman
creators of ZITS

HOW THE TEENAGER
KILLED TIME WHILE THE
INTERNET WAS DOWN.

Now arrange the circled letters to form
the surprise answer, as suggested by the
above cartoon.

*Print
answer
here*

" _____ "

JUMBLE®

Unscramble these four Jumbles, one letter
to each square, to form four ordinary words.

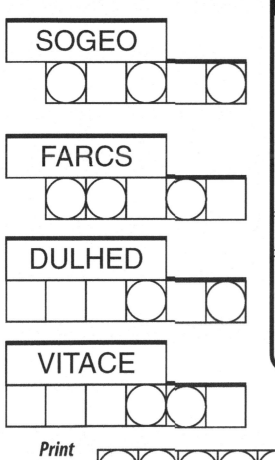

SOGEO

FARCS

DULHED

VITACE

Today's Guest JUMBLER is
MARIA SCRIVAN
creator of HALF FULL

WOULD YOU
LIKE TO HEAR
OUR SPECIALS?

THE ONLY REASON FIDO IS
ALLOWED IN A RESTAURANT
IS BECAUSE HE IS A ___

Now arrange the circled letters to form
the surprise answer, as suggested by the
above cartoon.

Print
answer
here

JUMBLE®

Unscramble these four Jumbles, one letter to each square, to form four ordinary words.

TUYOH

IYDEC

LARPIS

ASEWES

Today's Guest JUMBLER is
BRIAN CRANE
creator of PICKLES

ZZZ!

NAPPING CAME SO NATURALLY FOR HIM, HE COULD DO IT WITH _ _ _ _ _ _

Now arrange the circled letters to form the surprise answer, as suggested by the above cartoon.

Print answer here

JUMBLE®

Unscramble these four Jumbles, one letter to each square, to form four ordinary words.

RAGDU

OSMEO

RULSYE

NERLKE

Today's Guest JUMBLER is
MARK PARISI
creator of OFF THE MARK

STARTING LINE

WHAT THE STARTER SAID TO MY WIFE RIGHT BEFORE THE COUPLES' PIGGYBACK RACE.

Now arrange the circled letters to form the surprise answer, as suggested by the above cartoon.

Print answer here

JUMBLE®

Unscramble these four Jumbles, one letter
to each square, to form four ordinary words.

TABAE

SAHLS

ERRDAH

VIDLER

Today's Guest JUMBLER is
TOM RICHMOND
artist for MAD MAGAZINE

CHEWIE'S BIGGEST WORRY
ISN'T STORMTROOPERS
OR SITH LORDS... IT'S - - -

Now arrange the circled letters to form
the surprise answer, as suggested by the
above cartoon.

Print answer here

JUMBLE

Unscramble these four Jumbles, one letter to each square, to form four ordinary words.

NEYAH

TTCAR

LURBYR

UTDOGU

Today's Guest JUMBLER is
BILL KING co-creator of
MAC KING'S MAGIC IN A MINUTE

E-Z ROPE TRICK

I THINK I'VE ALMOST GOT IT!

TO LEARN HIS ROPE TRICKS,
THE MAGICIAN HAD...

Now arrange the circled letters to form the surprise answer, as suggested by the above cartoon.

Print answer here

" "

JUMBLE®

Unscramble these four Jumbles, one letter
to each square, to form four ordinary words.

UNANL

NKULF

DIDUGE

RIJYUN

I can't
change
another
quart.

Finish
this car
and call
it a day.

THE MECHANIC AT THE OIL
CHANGE PLACE WAS TIRED AT
THE END OF EACH DAY
BECAUSE HIS JOB WAS ---

Now arrange the circled letters to form
the surprise answer, as suggested by the
above cartoon.

Print answer here

JUMBLE®

Unscramble these four Jumbles, one letter to each square, to form four ordinary words.

LYSET

MENVO

VIRITA

MONCIE

Way to go!
One more time
from the top!

THE HIGH SCHOOL
CHEERLEADERS WERE SO
GOOD BECAUSE THEY
PRACTICED THEIR ---

Now arrange the circled letters to form the surprise answer, as suggested by the above cartoon.

Print answer
here "◯◯◯◯ - ◯◯◯◯◯"

JUMBLE®

Unscramble these four Jumbles, one letter
to each square, to form four ordinary words.

RAYRM

ESEGE

TORPYH

CIPAEE

I could watch shows about the moon all day.

We are live from Kennedy Space Center. The Apollo 11 mission has just lifted off.

WHEN THEY WATCHED THE APOLLO 11 MISSION ON TV, THEY WATCHED A ---

Now arrange the circled letters to form
the surprise answer, as suggested by the
above cartoon.

Print
answer
here

JUMBLE®

Unscramble these four Jumbles, one letter to each square, to form four ordinary words.

SUHLS

LIMYD

LEFWOL

HETGAR

Are you sure you don't want any turkey?

I'm good. I'll have some potatoes, yams and green beans. Oh, and rolls!

Cranberry sauce?

HE SKIPPED THE THANKSGIVING TURKEY, BUT FOOD WAS COMING TO HIM ---

Now arrange the circled letters to form the surprise answer, as suggested by the above cartoon.

Print answer here

JUMBLE®

Unscramble these four Jumbles, one letter
to each square, to form four ordinary words.

HNUCK

TURET

BIRSEC

PAJLOY

I really think I've found
my calling. I have a real
feel for this, don't you
think?

HE WANTED TO TELL THE
MASSEUSE THAT HE DIDN'T
LIKE HIS MASSAGE, BUT IT
MIGHT BE A ----

Now arrange the circled letters to form
the surprise answer, as suggested by the
above cartoon.

Print
answer
here

JUMBLE®

Unscramble these four Jumbles, one letter to each square, to form four ordinary words.

GEDWE

NITUP

WHYROT

HORYNT

The drywall is coming in two hours. Will you be finished?

I'll be cutting it close.

THE ELECTRICIAN WASN'T SURE HE'D FINISH IN TIME. IT WOULD COME ----

Now arrange the circled letters to form the surprise answer, as suggested by the above cartoon.

Print answer here

JUMBLE®

Unscramble these four Jumbles, one letter
to each square, to form four ordinary words.

KEHIR

DUMYD

CETINE

RAPORU

Why're you
playing D-B
minor-G-A
over and
over?

I'm just
trying to
memorize it.

THE GUITARIST THOUHT
UP A NEW MELODY AND,
TO REMEMBER IT, HE ----

Now arrange the circled letters to form
the surprise answer, as suggested by the
above cartoon.

Print
answer
here

" ☐☐ - ☐☐☐☐☐ - ☐☐ " ☐☐

JUMBLE®

Unscramble these four Jumbles, one letter
to each square, to form four ordinary words.

NOION

RNOWF

DIWYLL

GIWGEL

I've seen all his races.

I'll post that he's leading again.

I'm your biggest fan!

RUN TOM RUN

THE MARATHONER WON
RACE AFTER RACE AND
HAD A HUGE ----

Now arrange the circled letters to form
the surprise answer, as suggested by the
above cartoon.

Print answer here

JUMBLE®

Unscramble these four Jumbles, one letter
to each square, to form four ordinary words.

TYIFF

NATSD

PURNGS

GRUBRE

Little Jinxy keeps returning.

Aw, he likes you.

I'm allergic to cats.

THE CAT WAS DETERMINED
TO GET SOME ATTENTION
AND WAS BEING ----

Now arrange the circled letters to form
the surprise answer, as suggested by the
above cartoon.

Print
answer
here

" ⬡⬡⬡⬡⬡ - ⬡⬡⬡⬡⬡⬡⬡ "

JUMBLE®

Unscramble these four Jumbles, one letter to each square, to form four ordinary words.

CLOFA

CLERI

PIBSOH

GENTAM

Your usual, Norm?

Drinks for ALL my friends, Sammy!

Tomorrow, I'm buying.

THE REGULARS AT THE INSECT PUB WERE ----

Now arrange the circled letters to form the surprise answer, as suggested by the above cartoon.

Print answer here ◯◯◯ - ◯◯◯◯◯

JUMBLE®

Unscramble these four Jumbles, one letter
to each square, to form four ordinary words.

EMACO

SMURT

PLITUP

SUHAQS

You're
beautiful.
Would you
model for me?

Absolutely!
I'd love to.

WHEN THE ARTIST ASKED
TO MAKE A STONE LIKENESS
OF HER, SHE SAID ----

Now arrange the circled letters to form
the surprise answer, as suggested by the
above cartoon.

Print
answer
here

" ⬡⬡⬡⬡⬡⬡ - ⬡⬡⬡⬡ "

JUMBLE®

Unscramble these four Jumbles, one letter
to each square, to form four ordinary words.

BREDY

NARKD

GUNOLE

FOWULE

WHEN THE COUPLE FROM
SYDNEY PLANTED CARROTS
IN THEIR GARDEN, THEY
GREW ---

Now arrange the circled letters to form
the surprise answer, as suggested by the
above cartoon.

*Print answer
here*

JUMBLE®

Unscramble these four Jumbles, one letter
to each square, to form four ordinary words.

SOLPI

NALST

BAVEHE

CANYLU

Let's see. I have
another one: 56
minus 45.

57-39=

69-35=

100-45=

TO TEACH SUBTRACTION,
THE TEACHER HAD A ----

Now arrange the circled letters to form
the surprise answer, as suggested by the
above cartoon.

Print
answer
here   " ⬡⬡⬡⬡⬡⬡ "   ⬡⬡⬡⬡

JUMBLE®

Unscramble these four Jumbles, one letter to each square, to form four ordinary words.

SNIMU

LENKT

BUSDAR

TOIFUT

I need some more clarinet.

I'm glad you used John.

There's no one else who could do this.

WHEN IT CAME TO CREATING THE "STAR WARS" SOUNDTRACKS, JOHN WILLIAMS WAS ----

Now arrange the circled letters to form the surprise answer, as suggested by the above cartoon.

Print answer here

JUMBLE

Unscramble these four Jumbles, one letter to each square, to form four ordinary words.

RITYD

THURT

CADIZO

SOLONE

Isn't that where your photo was?

That is me! I just took out some wrinkles and added more hair.

THE SURGEON DIDN'T LIKE HIS PHOTO, SO HE ----

Now arrange the circled letters to form the surprise answer, as suggested by the above cartoon.

Print answer here

JUMBLE®

Unscramble these four Jumbles, one letter to each square, to form four ordinary words.

DUAIO

TELUF

DANDCI

WEERPT

Thanks! My wife needed the car and I really need to pump some iron today.

No problem. I'm pumped up.

JUMBLE GYM

THE BODYBUILDER ASKED HIS FRIEND FOR A RIDE TO THE GYM BECAUSE HE ----

Now arrange the circled letters to form the surprise answer, as suggested by the above cartoon.

Print answer here

JUMBLE®

Unscramble these four Jumbles, one letter to each square, to form four ordinary words.

VONEY

XORYP

TIFYES

GIDFIR

I thought you'd be hungry after repairing washers all day.

Look at all this. It's like Thanksgiving.

THE REPAIRMAN WAS ENJOYING HIS DINNER WITH ALL THE ----

Now arrange the circled letters to form the surprise answer, as suggested by the above cartoon.

Print answer here

JUMBLE®

Anniversary

Challenger Puzzles

JUMBLE®

Unscramble these six Jumbles, one letter to each square, to form six ordinary words.

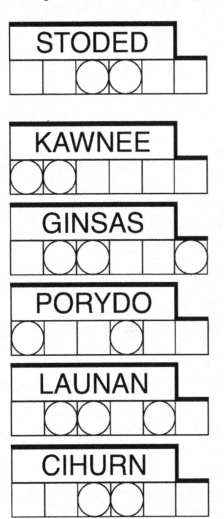

STODED

KAWNEE

GINSAS

PORYDO

LAUNAN

CIHURN

They need to update their site.

The clock we bought is still listed.

ANTIQUE TIMES

YESTERDAY'S TREASURES ARE HERE TODAY

1939 CLOCK

50% OFF!

I ♥ JUMBLE

THE ANTIQUE STORE'S WEBSITE FEATURED ---

Now arrange the circled letters to form the surprise answer, as suggested by the above cartoon.

Print answer here

164

JUMBLE.

Unscramble these six Jumbles, one letter to each square, to form six ordinary words.

CRIFEE

HRUYLO

KABSTE

NEDHIB

FIREUG

KANSHE

WHEN IT CAME TO WATCHING THE SUPER BOWL ON TV, THE PRE-GAME SHOW ----

Now arrange the circled letters to form the surprise answer, as suggested by the above cartoon.

Print answer here

JUMBLE®

Unscramble these six Jumbles, one letter to each square, to form six ordinary words.

SIFONU

SIRDAH

OEKOIC

DERNOT

RAWOND

SEPRUU

I thought the food would be twice as good. This is horrible.

This is the proper way to make meatballs!

I wouldn't play tennis with those. I know how to make meatballs!

WHEN THE RESTAURANT DECIDED TO HIRE TWO HEAD CHEFS, IT WAS A ----

Now arrange the circled letters to form the surprise answer, as suggested by the above cartoon.

Print answer here

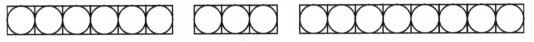

JUMBLE®

Unscramble these six Jumbles, one letter to each square, to form six ordinary words.

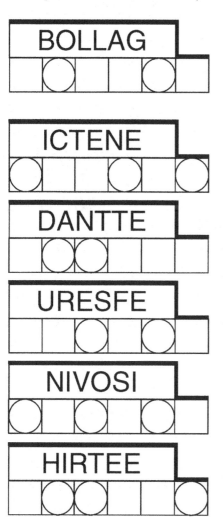

BOLLAG

ICTENE

DANTTE

URESFE

NIVOSI

HIRTEE

So, how does this work? I've never done this before. Ooh. He's cute.

I went here first when I was ready to start dating again.

LONELY HEARTS CLUB

SHE SIGNED UP FOR THE ONLINE DATING SERVICE IN THE HOPE OF ----

Now arrange the circled letters to form the surprise answer, as suggested by the above cartoon.

Print answer here

JUMBLE®

Unscramble these six Jumbles, one letter to each square, to form six ordinary words.

LIREOO

WETSEF

CANMEE

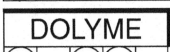

DOLYME

SPERUR

GRACEH

I can't sing in that key. That's it! I'm out of here. I don't need you.

I think it should be in G major.

THE SONGWRITER WAS REALLY UPSET WITH HIS SONGWRITING PARTNER AND NEEDED TO ---

Now arrange the circled letters to form the surprise answer, as suggested by the above cartoon.

Print answer here

JUMBLE®

Unscramble these six Jumbles, one letter to each square, to form six ordinary words.

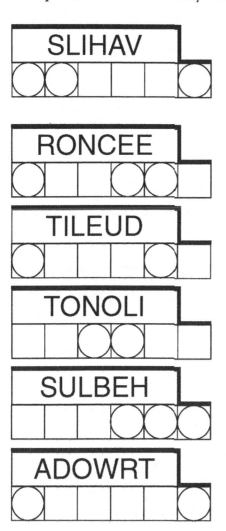

SLIHAV

RONCEE

TILEUD

TONOLI

SULBEH

ADOWRT

So, you're Zombie One. I'll be taking you out in the first scene. Be sure to duck or I'll hit you for real.

I can't tell you what an honor it is to be killed by you. I'm a big fan!

EVEN THOUGH HIS CHARACTER WOULD BE KILLED OFF QUICKLY, THE ACTOR WAS ---

Now arrange the circled letters to form the surprise answer, as suggested by the above cartoon.

Print answer here

JUMBLE®

Unscramble these six Jumbles, one letter to each square, to form six ordinary words.

LOTUWA

TOVMIE

PABUTE

KYSCIL

SPIMAH

TOARET

Wow! Not only does it look great, it's one of our best and we're practically giving it away today!

It's worth it to make my wife happy and to cover my bald spot.

GONE TODAY
HAIR TOMORROW

WITH THE HAIRPIECE ON SALE AT 70% OFF, HE CONSIDERED HIS PURCHASE TO BE A ----

Now arrange the circled letters to form the surprise answer, as suggested by the above cartoon.

Print answer here

☐☐☐☐☐ ☐☐☐☐☐☐ "☐☐☐☐☐☐"

JUMBLE®

Unscramble these six Jumbles, one letter to each square, to form six ordinary words.

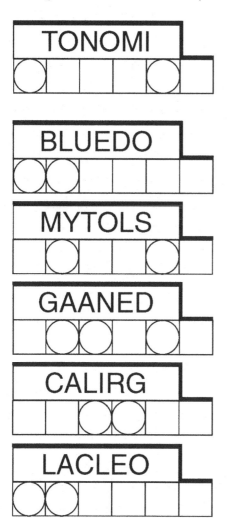

TONOMI

BLUEDO

MYTOLS

GAANED

CALIRG

LACLEO

They sure do look up to him.

They sure do.

Just reach out like you're shaking someone's hand.

Anything you say, Dad.

I did it, Dad! Just like you said to.

THE DAD WHO WENT BOWLING WITH HIS KIDS ON FATHER'S DAY WAS A ----

Now arrange the circled letters to form the surprise answer, as suggested by the above cartoon.

Print answer here

⬜⬜⬜⬜ "⬜⬜⬜⬜" ⬜⬜⬜⬜⬜

JUMBLE®

Unscramble these six Jumbles, one letter to each square, to form six ordinary words.

THIREM

FAYNIM

BOGNOL

BRAZEL

GLEEPD

LUDNYU

It would be cool to have matching cars.

Our dividends are off the charts!

You want two cars?

THE TWINS' STOCK MARKET INVESTMENTS MADE IT POSSIBLE FOR THEM TO ----

Now arrange the circled letters to form the surprise answer, as suggested by the above cartoon.

Print answer here

JUMBLE®

Unscramble these six Jumbles, one letter to each square, to form six ordinary words.

HNRUCC

WHORTG

TINKET

DYHRIB

QIEYUT

TARTOH

I've gained all my weight back. I need to start training for the Mini Marathon again.

I love you no matter what size you are. We'll train together.

HER HUSBAND STRUGGLED WITH HIS DIET FOR YEARS. SHE'S LOVED HIM ----

Now arrange the circled letters to form the surprise answer, as suggested by the above cartoon.

Print answer here

AND

JUMBLE®

Unscramble these six Jumbles, one letter to each square, to form six ordinary words.

KIFLEC

RAPORU

PORCEP

REELYC

FLYESM

CITANT

STUDIO 116

This isn't working. I'll have to photoshop some smiles in.

You two knock it off!

Keep going until we get it right!

IT WASN'T GOING TO BE EASY TO TAKE A FAMILY PHOTO THAT WAS ----

Now arrange the circled letters to form the surprise answer, as suggested by the above cartoon.

Print answer here

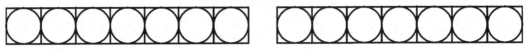

174

JUMBLE

Unscramble these six Jumbles, one letter to each square, to form six ordinary words.

GONEXY

YECLER

SADRIH

DOTNUL

DINDHE

TOONIM

What a brilliant coin.

It's a great likeness of the queen.

THEY THOUGHT PEOPLE WOULD LIKE THE NEW COIN WITH THE QUEEN'S PORTRAIT, AND THEY WERE ———

Now arrange the circled letters to form the surprise answer, as suggested by the above cartoon.

Print answer here

JUMBLE.

Unscramble these six Jumbles, one letter
to each square, to form six ordinary words.

TULIDE

NEREOC

SURFEE

BURTAP

GREVON

CEADFE

THE NEW ARCHERY RANGE
PUT UP A BILLBOARD TO
ADVERTISE TO THEIR ----

Now arrange the circled letters to form
the surprise answer, as suggested by the
above cartoon.

Print answer here

JUMBLE®

Unscramble these six Jumbles, one letter
to each square, to form six ordinary words.

DORHUS

DOLNOE

ZEHEWE

DUGTER

DUGELE

TPCIRS

THE BOXER WAS A SORE
LOSER. HE WASN'T THE KIND
OF BOXER TO ----

Now arrange the circled letters to form
the surprise answer, as suggested by the
above cartoon.

Print answer here

THE

Unscramble these six Jumbles, one letter to each square, to form six ordinary words.

HOTARU

TINEIF

CORGUH

NENTUL

VERIRD

AKENEW

No one has ever seen this formation. Our computer models show us advancing the ball, on average, 20 yards per play.

BoTron 2015

90% Success Potential.

They've got this down to a science.

94 · 15 · 15

THE OFFENSE WAS SO SUCCESSFUL BECAUSE THE COACH WAS ———

Now arrange the circled letters to form the surprise answer, as suggested by the above cartoon.

Print answer here

178

JUMBLE®

Unscramble these six Jumbles, one letter to each square, to form six ordinary words.

CRUSEP

PUBRAT

INTOGU

SAWELE

LULHIP

HADIRO

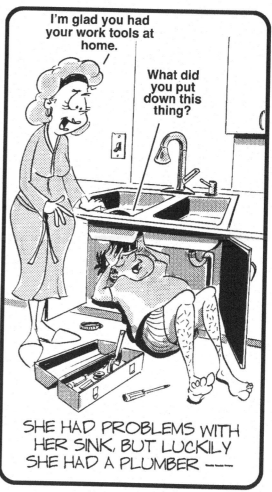

I'm glad you had your work tools at home.

What did you put down this thing?

SHE HAD PROBLEMS WITH HER SINK, BUT LUCKILY SHE HAD A PLUMBER ----

Now arrange the circled letters to form the surprise answer, as suggested by the above cartoon.

Print answer here

JUMBLE®

Unscramble these six Jumbles, one letter to each square, to form six ordinary words.

LIGYUT

RANWID

MENECT

DALHEN

BEETDA

RADPON

See? We had to raise our fees as more victims came forward.

And they call me a "bloodsucker."

VICTIMS

DRACULA'S LEGAL EXPENSES WERE ----

Now arrange the circled letters to form the surprise answer, as suggested by the above cartoon.

Print answer here

JUMBLE®

Unscramble these six Jumbles, one letter to each square, to form six ordinary words.

TIPRUN

FYDOLN

DUMLEO

TRMHYH

GAMTIS

KEYWEL

Sydney, you've outdone yourself.

I can see why she's considered the best!

There's no one hotter right now.

WHEN IT CAME TO DESIGNING BLOUSES, THE FASHION DESIGNER WAS ----

Now arrange the circled letters to form the surprise answer, as suggested by the above cartoon.

Print answer here

181

JUMBLE®

Unscramble these six Jumbles, one letter to each square, to form six ordinary words.

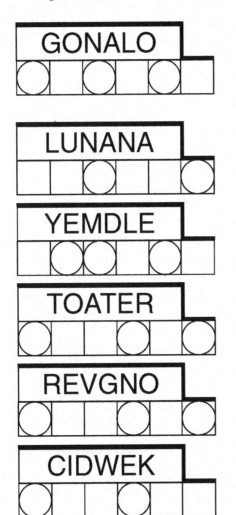

GONALO

LUNANA

YEMDLE

TOATER

REVGNO

CIDWEK

Way to go, sir!

I hear he'll get his star next week.

I knew he'd get it.

Congratulations on your promotion.

How does everybody know? They haven't announced it yet.

EVEN BEFORE THE COLONEL GOT HIS PROMOTION, IT WAS ----

Now arrange the circled letters to form the surprise answer, as suggested by the above cartoon.

Print answer here

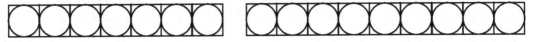

JUMBLE®

Unscramble these six Jumbles, one letter to each square, to form six ordinary words.

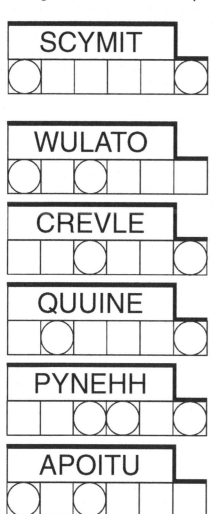

SCYMIT

WULATO

CREVLE

QUUINE

PYNEHH

APOITU

They keep communication going without having to say who and what every time.

HE HER HIM
I IT ME SHE
YOU THEY
US WE

Those?

There's a lot of these!

WHEN YOU SAY WORDS LIKE "I," "HE," "SHE," "HIM" AND "HER," YOU ----

Now arrange the circled letters to form the surprise answer, as suggested by the above cartoon.

Print answer here

Answers

1. **Jumbles:** TOPAZ LEECH OUTWIT CARPET
Answer: What the guy who swore he was going to lose weight ended up eating—"CROW"

2. **Jumbles:** SOOTY HOIST CUPFUL MODEST
Answer: What a cat burglar must never do—PUSSYFOOT

3. **Jumbles:** FROZE SNOWY HOMAGE ENTICE
Answer: Said with a smile—CHEESE

4. **Jumbles:** FIORD CHAMP GENDER BECKON
Answer: What that old goat acted like—A "KID"

5. **Jumbles:** LOGIC GUARD GROUCH DEVICE
Answer: "When she said I could make her 'mine,' I knew she was this"—"A GOLD DIGGER"

6. **Jumbles:** ARBOR FLOUT BUREAU LOCKET
Answer: If you're suffering from laryngitis, you'd best not do this—TALK ABOUT IT

7. **Jumbles:** STUNG GORGE BUSHEL AWHILE
Answer: The pessimist hung around the delicatessen looking for this—THE "WURST"

8. **Jumbles:** PAPER BROOK REVERE CLAUSE
Answer: What they called the music librarian—THE SCOREKEEPER

9. **Jumbles:** LUCID CHASM BABOON EQUITY
Answer: Should you cut them and throw them away—or just file them?—NAILS

10. **Jumbles:** PROVE CLOTH FRACAS TEMPER
Answer: What that TV show about skiing turned out to be—A "SLOPE" OPERA

11. **Jumbles:** POUND QUASH LOUNGE FARINA
Answer: What they called the beautician—THE "PAN-HANDLER"

12. **Jumbles:** FEVER MANLY BAKERY HEALTH
Answer: What they called that classy new art gallery—THE HALL OF FAME

13. **Jumbles:** BLESS DOWDY PONCHO CURFEW
Answer: What the kid who said he didn't like alphabet soup ended up eating—HIS OWN WORDS

14. **Jumbles:** PUTTY STAID ANYONE RAMROD
Answer: What the invisible man's mother or father must have been—A "TRANS-PARENT"

15. **Jumbles:** ENSUE FATAL CARBON JURIST
Answer: He tried to compose a drinking song but didn't make it past this—THE FIRST 2 BARS

16. **Jumbles:** CLOAK MINER CABANA HECTIC
Answer: Those famous sculptures were sure something to this—"MARBLE" AT

17. **Jumbles:** CURRY BOUGH AFRAID MUFFLE
Answer: What you might see if you refuse her request for a mink coat—THE FUR FLY

18. **Jumbles:** IGLOO CHAOS GARLIC BARREN
Answer: What kind of a place was that rabbit farm?—"HARE-RAISING"

19. **Jumbles:** AWFUL HEDGE TIMELY FEEBLE
Answer: What's a cattle rustler?—A BEEF THIEF

20. **Jumbles:** QUAIL HAREM RATHER ASSURE
Answer: What the broken photograph record must have been—A SMASH HIT

21. **Jumbles:** BALKY FORUM EROTIC MALTED
Answer: He sold his products to the pickle factory—THE FARMER IN THE "DILL"

22. **Jumbles:** BASIS AFOOT BICKER SPLEEN
Answer: What a good tongue sandwich should do—SPEAK FOR ITSELF

23. **Jumbles:** CROWN MADAM BELFRY LIMBER
Answer: His autobiography showed that the only thing wrong with the author was this—HIS MEMORY

24. **Jumbles:** CHEEK ABIDE EXTANT SUNDAE
Answer: How dogs who chase cars sometimes end up—"EXHAUST-ED"

25. **Jumbles:** CLOUT DECAY BEAUTY SQUIRM
Answer: Weight lifters in restaurants—CALORIES

26. **Jumbles:** ARDOR USURP UNLIKE VALUED
Answer: On a wet day, this is where they held a huddle—IN A PUDDLE

27. **Jumbles:** BEFOG CURVE AFFRAY PENMAN
Answer: What do you get when you use soap and water on the stove?—FOAM ON THE RANGE

28. **Jumbles:** PERKY MAGIC DOOMED RENEGE
Answer: What to say to someone who complains of being a light sleeper—TRY DOING IT IN THE DARK

29. **Jumbles:** LOOSE CLOVE BRUTAL POPLIN
Answer: That cemetery was under heavy security because of this—ALL THE "PLOTS" THERE

30. **Jumbles:** JULEP FAVOR INDICT CORNER
Answer: What getting to a picnic often is not—A PICNIC

31. **Jumbles:** BRAWL THYME FINITE PAUNCH
Answer: That eccentric hen sat on an ax so she could do this—"HATCH-ET"

32. **Jumbles:** ACRID LOUSE BAUBLE EVOLVE
Answer: What too much champagne can make a single person do—SEE DOUBLE

33. **Jumbles:** VAGUE CATCH TREATY WAITER
Answer: What that guy who was always letting a smile be his umbrella ended up with—WET TEETH

34. **Jumbles:** BOOTH DUSKY SCORCH FOIBLE
Answer: What a man who plants his feet firmly in the ground sometimes gets—DIRTY SHOES

35. **Jumbles:** HOARD PEONY MOBILE DEFILE
Answer: How to get a guy to donate to the blood bank—"NEEDLE" HIM

36. **Jumbles:** FROZE AXIOM BUTLER SCURVY
Answer: What a man who tries to act like a tough cookie often does when push comes to shove—CRUMBLES

37. **Jumbles:** BANAL ADAGE ENOUGH ALIGHT
Answer: She accepted his proposal because he was this type of a guy—AN "ENGAGING" ONE

38. **Jumbles:** DEMON PANIC ARTFUL USEFUL
Answer: What the tow truck was trying to do at the auto race—PULL A FAST ONE

39. **Jumbles:** COLIC HOIST ENCAMP BOLERO
Answer: What pierces your ear without leaving a hole?—NOISE

40. **Jumbles:** FUROR TROTH BLAZER INDIGO
Answer: What an exciting "match" will do for the fans—LIGHT A FIRE

41. **Jumbles:** ICING BALMY GIBLET APIECE
Answer: He told them he was just what the doctor ordered—A BIG PILL

42. **Jumbles:** PARKA HENNA THIRTY JERSEY
Answer: The man who marries for money will usually have to do this—EARN IT

43. **Jumbles:** CRAZE ENJOY ZITHER WISDOM
Answer: What they called that very clever oil tycoon—THE WIZARD OF "OOZE"

44. **Jumbles:** BEGUN PHONY HANSOM ARCTIC
Answer: Some men make money without working for it from suckers who want to do this—THE SAME THING

45. **Jumbles:** AVAIL TARRY EMBRYO ROTATE
Answer: How cross-examination is sometimes conducted—BY TRIAL & TERROR

184

46. **Jumbles:** BURLY IGLOO OBTUSE UNSAID
Answer: Some kids who are tall enough to drive the family car are too short to do this—BUY THE GAS

47. **Jumbles:** MOLDY GROOM ATTACH LEEWAY
Answer: What air pollution is—NO EARTHLY GOOD

48. **Jumbles:** COCOA LATCH WATERY PUNDIT
Answer: When dinners are quickly thought out these days, they're often this—THAWED OUT

49. **Jumbles:** PANSY APRON BISECT HEAVEN
Answer: Another name for "hors d'oeuvres"—"APPE-TEASERS"

50. **Jumbles:** OZONE LURID FORGER PEOPLE
Answer: What the cave art might be a primitive form of—DEEP "FRIEZE"

51. **Jumbles:** GRAVE ASSAY RADIAL TYCOON
Answer: Many after-dinner speakers are inclined to give you more than this—YOU CAN DIGEST

52. **Jumbles:** VENOM CREEK HAGGLE UNFAIR
Answer: There are some women who don't object to men who "love 'em and leave 'em"—providing the men do this—LEAVE 'EM ENOUGH

53. **Jumbles:** BUXOM FOUNT STUDIO INWARD
Answer: What the bill collector said after a rewarding day's work—WHAT'S "DUN" IS "DUN"

54. **Jumbles:** SWOOP BISON STOLEN ASSURE
Answer: A collector usually has an obsession with this—POSSESSION

55. **Jumbles:** BULLY LATHE MARROW WALRUS
Answer: How the manufacturer wanted to make money—IN THE "WURST" WAY

56. **Jumbles:** PROVE OLDER HIATUS SECEDE
Answer: What a good salesman knows how to bring—ORDERS OUT OF CHAOS

57. **Jumbles:** BOWER FLANK BECALM ZINNIA
Answer: Where there's a will there's sometimes this—A WAIL

58. **Jumbles:** GRIMY CHANT TALLOW SWERVE
Answer: People who are too anxious to make a living have sometimes forgotten this—HOW TO LIVE

59. **Jumbles:** PECAN BLIMP BEMOAN VISION
Answer: The jogger visited the veterinarian because of this—HIS "CALVES" WERE IN PAIN

60. **Jumbles:** AMITY DUNCE SLUICE MURMUR
Answer: What the organ grinder had—A "TURN" FOR MUSIC

61. **Jumbles:** MERCY HOUSE BLOTCH FILTHY
Answer: If her husband didn't buckle up while driving, she was going to—BELT HIM

62. **Jumbles:** BRAVE MERGE SAILOR WALNUT
Answer: The monsters' toddler wouldn't be hideous enough to scare people until he—GREW SOME

63. **Jumbles:** KNIFE GLINT TATTLE TROPHY
Answer: His diet and exercise program succeeded. He lost weight because he didn't—TAKE IT LIGHTLY

64. **Jumbles:** METAL BASIS BRUNCH WALLOP
Answer: The fashion shoot featured a model dressed as a hitchhiker with—"A-POSABLE" THUMB

65. **Jumbles:** ANNOY SEIZE VANITY FLAUNT
Answer: Storm chasers who are too intent on getting close to a twister have—"FUNNEL" VISION

66. **Jumbles:** HEAVY TEASE IMPALA CONVOY
Answer: He would be hired as their new sneakers salesman because he was a—"SHOE"-IN

67. **Jumbles:** BRAVO MUSIC WORKED UPBEAT
Answer: When they added up their strokes on the golf hole, they were a—"TWO-SOME"

68. **Jumbles:** RELIC EVOKE FAÇADE RITUAL
Answer: If you thought the center of the earth was as hot as the surface of the sun, you'd be—"CORE-ECT"

69. **Jumbles:** BUNNY PANDA DUGOUT ADMIRE
Answer: With the weekend over, the Jumble creators started working on—"PUNDAY" MORNING

70. **Jumbles:** AISLE ALIAS MAGNUM INVADE
Answer: It was dinnertime after a long day of planting bushes and he was ready to—DIG IN

71. **Jumbles:** ADULT SCOUR PAGODA MAINLY
Answer: He didn't buy the abacus because he wanted one without—ADD-ONS

72. **Jumbles:** NINTH RAINY SAVORY UNTRUE
Answer: When it came to Thomas Edison's innovations, the museum had an impressive—INVENT-ORY

73. **Jumbles:** STUNT STYLE UNIQUE BEAKER
Answer: Getting a cash advance on his credit card wasn't in his—BEST INTEREST

74. **Jumbles:** FLIRT DOUSE RUNOFF TETHER
Answer: Both houses were for lease, and their decision would be based on the—"DIFFER-RENTS"

75. **Jumbles:** SPENT NOSEY SPRAIN SUBURB
Answer: When the Jumble creators appeared at the live event, everyone enjoyed their—"PUNNY" BUSINESS

76. **Jumbles:** KITTY JUICE QUIVER POMPOM
Answer: Building an elaborate doghouse in the backyard was his—PET PROJECT

77. **Jumbles:** ANKLE NOTCH ABSORB BISQUE
Answer: If Christmas was held on March 17, then we'd get—"SAINT-O'-CLAUS"

78. **Jumbles:** GAUDY ABACK ACTUAL BALLOT
Answer: The firewood business was doing so well that there was a—BACKLOG

79. **Jumbles:** WAFER RUMMY SPOOKY FONDLY
Answer: The inventor of the felt tip pen said, "These will be a big hit,—MARK MY WORDS"

80. **Jumbles:** GUILT EVENT GOVERN FORBID
Answer: There wasn't a cloud in the sky when the new king began—REIGNING

81. **Jumbles:** HIKER GLOAT SAFARI BAMBOO
Answer: After carelessly puncturing all four tires, he would be—FLAT BROKE

82. **Jumbles:** DECAY OZONE EXPIRE SPRAIN
Answer: It was time to plant the corn, and the farmer was ready to—"PRO-SEED"

83. **Jumbles:** PERCH LEMUR CAMERA BOTANY
Answer: After discovering fraud at the aerospace company, they would need to—LAUNCH A PROBE

84. **Jumbles:** ROBOT LOGIC LEEWAY MEMBER
Answer: When it came to not telling the truth, he was—"RE-LIE-ABLE"

85. **Jumbles:** FABLE TENET HAIRDO IMPOSE
Answer: Their kite flew so well because it was—TOP-OF-THE-LINE

86. **Jumbles:** RALLY WOUND EFFECT RHYTHM
Answer: He specialized in building secure structures for troops. It was his—FORTE

87. **Jumbles:** SOUPY SKIER TOPPLE VACUUM
Answer: The universe is home to so many planets, stars and galaxies because it's—OUTER SPACIOUS

88. **Jumbles:** MOURN HOIST SHREWD SPRUCE
Answer: His rival at the hot air balloon race—SHOWED HIM UP

89. **Jumbles:** ELUDE YIELD GEYSER ABOUND
Answer: He told stories about the cow that had produced so much milk because she was—"LEGEND-DAIRY"

90. **Jumbles:** RUMMY HOARD GENIUS INHALE
Answer: The comedian wasn't all that funny. When a few people laughed, they were—HUMORING HIM

91. **Jumbles:** VERGE HATCH GLANCE ABSURD
Answer: She was struggling to learn sign language, so the instructor—GAVE HER A HAND

92. **Jumbles:** OZONE DIRTY CHOSEN DECEIT
Answer: He asked his wife if he could play craps, but she said—NO DICE

93. **Jumbles:** SHAKY MORPH OUTAGE BOBBLE
Answer: The customers at the fireworks store were—BABY BOOMERS

94. **Jumbles:** WAGER MUDDY ASSURE BOUNCE
Answer: When he showed his wife the abacus he'd bought, she thought it was—"AWE-SUM"

95. **Jumbles:** SWOON SPURN DOODLE IGUANA
Answer: He was explaining to the climber that being a Sherpa had its—UPS AND DOWNS

96. **Jumbles:** PENNY MAMBO WHIMSY DEFIED
Answer: He couldn't remember what time the sun would rise, but then it—DAWNED ON HIM

97. **Jumbles:** RIVER FINCH PURSUE REVERT
Answer: One ghost didn't fit in with the rest because he was a—FREE SPIRIT

98. **Jumbles:** PANSY SHINY WETTER PAGODA
Answer: After a tiger escaped from the zoo, there would be this until there was this.—APPREHENSION

99. **Jumbles:** GIANT IMPEL RODENT SHOULD
Answer: When neighbors helped them install their new landscaping, they had a—SHINDIG

100. **Jumbles:** PLUMB RURAL ACCENT BOUNTY
Answer: They could sail their new boat from Key West to Miami to Boston because it was—PORT-ABLE

101. **Jumbles:** OCTET STRUM CHROME WEAKLY
Answer: The dairy farmer was making huge profits. He loved his—CASH COW

102. **Jumbles:** GRIEF KNIFE LAGOON LAPTOP
Answer: When it came to whether or not she'd be able to keep a secret, there was—NO TELLING

103. **Jumbles:** DUNCE TALLY GROOVY ROSIER
Answer: The invention of the wheel was—REVOLUTIONARY

104. **Jumbles:** CIVIL ICING POLLEN PURELY
Answer: Being the principal of a high school had seemed like such a good idea,—IN PRINCIPLE

105. **Jumbles:** GIVEN SHEEN BEHIND ASTHMA
Answer: He had bushes to block out his neighbors, but he planted some more to—HEDGE HIS BETS

106. **Jumbles:** TWINE IRONY WINERY INVEST
Answer: The twins had incredible powers of perception. They were very—"IN-TWO-ITIVE"

107. **Jumbles:** FORGO HUSKY LENGTH GLANCE
Answer: He'd planned to cut the tree down without any problems, but his plans—FELL THROUGH

108. **Jumbles:** HOIST METAL GOALIE NIMBLE
Answer: The retired army general tried to lose weight, but it was a—LOSING BATTLE

109. **Jumbles:** TIGER THEFT ROOKIE OUTLET
Answer: When the stallion noticed the attractive mare in the pasture, he was—HOT TO TROT

110. **Jumbles:** TRACK WHARF ENCORE METRIC
Answer: The sofa the dog slept on was in rough shape because of all the—WEAR AND "TERRIER"

111. **Jumbles:** SWEPT BASIS ACTUAL DIVERT
Answer: The undercover cop bought the Rolex from the street vendor because—IT WAS A STEAL

112. **Jumbles:** SCARF LUCKY ATTAIN POLICY
Answer: Everyone loved Leonard Nimoy's role as a Vulcan and thought he was—"SPOCKTACULAR"

113. **Jumbles:** FLASK AROSE DELUXE OUTLET
Answer: When it came to training for races, the sprinter was—STEADFAST

114. **Jumbles:** MOUND RANCH SLEEPY WILLOW
Answer: When the "punny" guy was asked if he'd like to go to the beach, he said—I "SHORE" WOULD

115. **Jumbles:** BIRCH ADOPT EITHER RABBIT
Answer: The physical therapist's office was a little run-down, so she—REHABBED IT

116. **Jumbles:** TROLL SHOWN OCTANE DENOTE
Answer: The pioneering couple argued about which tract of land to build on and couldn't—SETTLE ON ONE

117. **Jumbles:** AGILE RODEO TAVERN CANNON
Answer: The hypnotist made a—GRAND EN-TRANCE

118. **Jumbles:** EVOKE APPLY SEASON REVOLT
Answer: Her cat and dog were high maintenance because they had so many—PET PEEVES

119. **Jumbles:** ABIDE HEFTY EMBLEM DISMAL
Answer: When it came to buying weather stripping, the fact that it was on sale—SEALED THE DEAL

120. **Jumbles:** HABIT HIKER CACKLE BOTTLE
Answer: The mother bird transported her eggs in a—HATCHBACK

121. **Jumbles:** DECAY SPELL WRITER HUNGRY
Answer: The identity of the mummy was—UNDER WRAPS

122. **Jumbles:** SOUPY USHER SCENIC YONDER
Answer: The drummer's tell-all autobiography had—REPERCUSSIONS

123. **Jumbles:** OOMPH DOILY SICKLY BESIDE
Answer: The library was having a series of authors speak and was—BOOKED SOLID

124. **Jumbles:** USURP ELOPE DONKEY UTOPIA
Answer: The harbormaster was a little overweight, but his wife liked him on the—PORTLY SIDE

125. **Jumbles:** OPERA WITTY SLOWLY DREDGE
Answer: When she started to give out extra candy, the trick-or-treaters thought it was a—SWEET DEAL

126. **Jumbles:** HAPPY PLUCK TACKLE HECTIC
Answer: The movers had no problems lifting the heavy boxes, but she wanted them to—PICK UP THE PACE

127. **Jumbles:** ORBIT WORLD LIKELY LIQUID
Answer: After discovering oil on their property, they would become—WELL-TO-DO

128. **Jumbles:** INEPT RATIO ONWARD OPAQUE
Answer: The cowboy didn't want to participate in the rodeo, but he got—ROPED INTO IT

129. **Jumbles:** HAVOC GRIEF RATHER THIRST
Answer: The fancy new weather balloon was—HIGH-TECH

130. **Jumbles:** DOUSE FLOOD ADRIFT ACQUIT
Answer: The violinist went to the doctor because he wasn't—FIT AS A FIDDLE

131. **Jumbles:** GLAZE MUDDY OPENLY CLAMOR
Answer: He had too much cake for his 18th birthday and was now a—"GROAN"-UP

132. **Jumbles:** KIOSK TREND GROUND HARBOR
Answer: The prison inmate used acne cream because he was—BREAKING OUT

133. **Jumbles:** KITTY LOGIC LOTION ASTRAY
Answer: The handsome bowler was—STRIKING

134. **Jumbles:** DAISY AROSE DRENCH ACCORD
Answer: When his girlfriend broke up with him on Friday, the weekend started on a —"SADDER-DAY"

135. **Jumbles:** KNIFE TWEAK DRESSY AVIARY
Answer: Mick and Keith worked on "(I Can't Get No) Satisfaction" until they—WERE SATISFIED

136. **Jumbles:** STOMP ELDER ACCEPT HAIRDO
Answer: The fashion model didn't like her new competition and thought she—POSED A THREAT

137. **Jumbles:** FILMY CLANG FIASCO SPRAIN
Answer: He played QB in high school, college and now the NFL because being a QB wasn't a—PASSING FANCY

138. **Jumbles:** TREND GRIND MAYHEM ACCESS
Answer: How the teenager killed time while the Internet was down—"DAYSTREAMING"

139. **Jumbles:** GOOSE SCARF HUDDLE ACTIVE
Answer: The only reason Fido is allowed in a restaurant is because he is a—SERVICE DOG

140. **Jumbles:** YOUTH DICEY SPIRAL SEESAW
Answer: Napping came so naturally for him, he could do it with—HIS EYES CLOSED

141. **Jumbles:** GUARD MOOSE SURELY KERNEL
Answer: What the starter said to my wife right before the couples' piggyback race—ON YOUR MARK

142. **Jumbles:** ABATE SLASH HARDER DRIVEL
Answer: Chewie's biggest worry isn't Stormtroopers or Sith Lords… It's—HAIRBALLS

143. **Jumbles:** HYENA TRACT BLURRY DUGOUT
Answer: To learn his rope tricks, the magician had—TO BE "TAUT"

144. **Jumbles:** ANNUL FLUNK GUIDED INJURY
Answer: The mechanic at the oil change place was tired at the end of each day because his job was—DRAINING

145. **Jumbles:** STYLE VENOM TRIVIA INCOME
Answer: The high school cheerleaders were so good because they practiced their—"ROOT-TEENS"

146. **Jumbles:** MARRY GEESE TROPHY APIECE
Answer: When they watched the Apollo 11 mission on TV, they watched a—SPACE PROGRAM

147. **Jumbles:** SLUSH DIMLY FELLOW GATHER
Answer: He skipped the Thanksgiving turkey, but food was coming to him—FROM ALL SIDES

148. **Jumbles:** CHUNK UTTER SCRIBE JALOPY
Answer: He wanted totell the masseuse that he didn't like his massage, but it might be a—TOUCHY SUBJECT

149. **Jumbles:** WEDGE INPUT WORTHY THORNY
Answer: The electrician wasn't sure he'd finish in time. It would come—DOWN TO THE WIRE

150. **Jumbles:** HIKER MUDDY ENTICE UPROAR
Answer: The guitarist thought up a new melody and, to remember it, he—"RE-CHORD-ED" IT

151. **Jumbles:** ONION FROWN WILDLY WIGGLE
Answer: The marathoner won race after race and had a huge—FOLLOWING

152. **Jumbles:** FIFTY STAND SPRUNG BURGER
Answer: The cat was determined to get some attention and was being—"PURR-SISTENT"

153. **Jumbles:** FOCAL RELIC BISHOP MAGNET
Answer: The regulars at the insect pub were—BAR-FLIES

154. **Jumbles:** CAMEO STRUM PULPIT SQUASH
Answer: When the artist asked to make a stone likeness of her, she said—"SCULPT-SURE"

155. **Jumbles:** DERBY DRANK LOUNGE WOEFUL
Answer: When the couple from Sydney planted carrots in their garden, they grew—DOWN UNDER

156. **Jumbles:** SPOIL SLANT BEHAVE LUNACY
Answer: To teach subtraction, the teacher had a—"LESSEN" PLAN

157. **Jumbles:** MINUS KNELT ABSURD OUTFIT
Answer: When it came to creating the "Star Wars" soundtracks, John Williams was—INSTRUMENTAL

158. **Jumbles:** DIRTY TRUTH ZODIAC LOOSEN
Answer: The surgeon didn't like his photo so he—DOCTORED IT

159. **Jumbles:** AUDIO FLUTE CANDID PEWTER
Answer: The bodybuilder asked his friend for a ride to the gym because he—NEEDED A LIFT

160. **Jumbles:** ENVOY PROXY FEISTY FRIGID
Answer: The repairman was enjoying his dinner with all the—FIXIN'S

161. **Jumbles:** ODDEST WEAKEN ASSIGN DROOPY ANNUAL URCHIN
Answer: The antique store's website featured—SECONDHAND NEWS

162. **Jumbles:** FIERCE HOURLY BASKET BEHIND FIGURE SHAKEN
Answer: When it came to watching the Super Bowl on TV, the pre-game show—KICKED THINGS OFF

163. **Jumbles:** FUSION RADISH COOKIE RODENT ONWARD PURSUE
Answer: When the restaurant decided to hire two head chefs, it was a—RECIPE FOR DISASTER

164. **Jumbles:** GLOBAL ENTICE ATTEND REFUSE VISION EITHER
Answer: She signed up for the online dating service in the hope of—LOVE AT FIRST "SITE"

165. **Jumbles:** ORIOLE FEWEST MENACE MELODY PURSER CHARGE
Answer: The songwriter was really upset with his songwriting partner and needed to—COMPOSE HIMSELF

166. **Jumbles:** LAVISH ENCORE DILUTE LOTION BUSHEL TOWARD
Answer: Even though his character would be killed off quickly, the actor was—THRILLED TO DEATH

167. **Jumbles:** OUTLAW MOTIVE UPBEAT SICKLY MISHAP ROTATE
Answer: With the hairpiece on sale at 70% off, he considered his purchase to be a—SMALL PRICE "TOUPEE"

168. **Jumbles:** MOTION DOUBLE MOSTLY AGENDA GARLIC LOCALE
Answer: The dad who went bowling with his kinds on Father's Day was a—GOOD "ROLL" MODEL

169. **Jumbles:** HERMIT INFAMY OBLONG BLAZER PLEDGE UNDULY
Answer: The twins' stock market investments made it possible for them to—DOUBLE THEIR MONEY

170. **Jumbles:** CRUNCH GROWTH KITTEN HYBRID EQUITY THROAT
Answer: Her husband struggled with his diet for years. She's loved him—THROUGH THICK AND THIN

171. **Jumbles:** FICKLE UPROAR COPPER CELERY MYSELF INTACT
Answer: It wasn't going to be easy to take a family photo that was—PICTURE PERFECT

172. **Jumbles:** OXYGEN CELERY RADISH UNTOLD HIDDEN MOTION
Answer: They thought people would like the new coin with the queen's portrait, and they were—RIGHT ON THE MONEY

173. **Jumbles:** DILUTE ENCORE REFUSE ABRUPT GOVERN DEFACE
Answer: The new archery range put up a billboard to advertise to their—TARGET AUDIENCE

174. **Jumbles:** SHROUD NOODLE WHEEZE TRUDGE DELUGE SCRIPT
Answer: The boxer was a sore loser. He wasn't the kind of boxer to—ROLL WITH THE PUNCHES

175. **Jumbles:** AUTHOR FINITE GROUCH TUNNEL DRIVER WEAKEN
Answer: The offense was so successful because the coach was—FORWARD THINKING

176. **Jumbles:** SPRUCE ABRUPT OUTING WEASEL UPHILL HAIRDO
Answer: She had problems with her sink, but luckily she had a plumber—AT HER DISPOSAL

177. **Jumbles:** GUILTY INWARD CEMENT HANDLE DEBATE PARDON
Answer: Dracula's legal expenses were—BLEEDING HIM DRY

178. **Jumbles:** TURNIP FONDLY MODULE RHYTHM STIGMA WEEKLY
Answer: When it came to designing blouses, the fashion designer was—TOPS IN HER FIELD

179. **Jumbles:** LAGOON ANNUAL MEDLEY ROTATE GOVERN WICKED
Answer: Even before the colonel got his promotion, it was—GENERAL KNOWLEDGE

180. **Jumbles:** MYSTIC OUTLAW CLEVER UNIQUE HYPHEN UTOPIA
Answer: When you say words like "I," "he," "she," "him" and "her," you—PRONOUN-CE THEM

Need More Jumbles®?

Order any of these books through your bookseller or call Triumph Books toll-free at 800-888-4741.

Jumble® Books

More than 175 puzzles each!

Cowboy Jumble®
$10.95 • ISBN: 978-1-62937-355-3

Jammin' Jumble®
$9.95 • ISBN: 978-1-57243-844-6

Java Jumble®
$10.95 • ISBN: 978-1-60078-415-6

Jet Set Jumble®
$9.95 • ISBN: 978-1-60078-353-1

Jolly Jumble®
$10.95 • ISBN: 978-1-60078-214-5

Jumble® Anniversary
$10.95 • ISBN: 987-1-62937-734-6

Jumble® Ballet
$10.95 • ISBN: 978-1-62937-616-5

Jumble® Birthday
$10.95 • ISBN: 978-1-62937-652-3

Jumble® Celebration
$10.95 • ISBN: 978-1-60078-134-6

Jumble® Champion
$10.95 • ISBN: 978-1-62937-870-1

Jumble® Cuisine
$10.95 • ISBN: 978-1-62937-735-3

Jumble® Drag Race
$9.95 • ISBN: 978-1-62937-483-3

Jumble® Ever After
$10.95 • ISBN: 978-1-62937-785-8

Jumble® Explorer
$9.95 • ISBN: 978-1-60078-854-3

Jumble® Explosion
$10.95 • ISBN: 978-1-60078-078-3

Jumble® Fever
$9.95 • ISBN: 978-1-57243-593-3

Jumble® Galaxy
$10.95 • ISBN: 978-1-60078-583-2

Jumble® Garden
$10.95 • ISBN: 978-1-62937-653-0

Jumble® Genius
$10.95 • ISBN: 978-1-57243-896-5

Jumble® Geography
$10.95 • ISBN: 978-1-62937-615-8

Jumble® Getaway
$10.95 • ISBN: 978-1-60078-547-4

Jumble® Gold
$10.95 • ISBN: 978-1-62937-354-6

Jumble® Jackpot
$10.95 • ISBN: 978-1-57243-897-2

Jumble® Jailbreak
$9.95 • ISBN: 978-1-62937-002-6

Jumble® Jambalaya
$9.95 • ISBN: 978-1-60078-294-7

Jumble® Jitterbug
$10.95 • ISBN: 978-1-60078-584-9

Jumble® Journey
$10.95 • ISBN: 978-1-62937-549-6

Jumble® Jubilation
$10.95 • ISBN: 978-1-62937-784-1

Jumble® Jubilee
$10.95 • ISBN: 978-1-57243-231-4

Jumble® Juggernaut
$9.95 • ISBN: 978-1-60078-026-4

Jumble® Kingdom
$10.95 • ISBN: 978-1-62937-079-8

Jumble® Knockout
$9.95 • ISBN: 978-1-62937-078-1

Jumble® Madness
$10.95 • ISBN: 978-1-892049-24-7

Jumble® Magic
$9.95 • ISBN: 978-1-60078-795-9

Jumble® Mania
$10.95 • ISBN: 978-1-57243-697-8

Jumble® Marathon
$9.95 • ISBN: 978-1-60078-944-1

Jumble® Neighbor
$10.95 • ISBN: 978-1-62937-845-9

Jumble® Parachute
$10.95 • ISBN: 978-1-62937-548-9

Jumble® Safari
$9.95 • ISBN: 978-1-60078-675-4

Jumble® Sensation
$10.95 • ISBN: 978-1-60078-548-1

Jumble® Skyscraper
$10.95 • ISBN: 978-1-62937-869-5

Jumble® Symphony
$10.95 • ISBN: 978-1-62937-131-3

Jumble® Theater
$9.95 • ISBN: 978-1-62937-484-0

Jumble® University
$10.95 • ISBN: 978-1-62937-001-9

Jumble® Unleashed
$10.95 • ISBN: 978-1-62937-844-2

Jumble® Vacation
$10.95 • ISBN: 978-1-60078-796-6

Jumble® Wedding
$9.95 • ISBN: 978-1-62937-307-2

Jumble® Workout
$10.95 • ISBN: 978-1-60078-943-4

Jump, Jive and Jumble®
$9.95 • ISBN: 978-1-60078-215-2

Lunar Jumble®
$9.95 • ISBN: 978-1-60078-853-6

Monster Jumble®
$10.95 • ISBN: 978-1-62937-213-6

Mystic Jumble®
$9.95 • ISBN: 978-1-62937-130-6

Rainy Day Jumble®
$10.95 • ISBN: 978-1-60078-352-4

Royal Jumble®
$10.95 • ISBN: 978-1-60078-738-6

Sports Jumble®
$10.95 • ISBN: 978-1-57243-113-3

Summer Fun Jumble®
$10.95 • ISBN: 978-1-57243-114-0

Touchdown Jumble®
$9.95 • ISBN: 978-1-62937-212-9

Oversize Jumble® Books

More than 500 puzzles!

Colossal Jumble®
$19.95 • ISBN: 978-1-57243-490-5

Jumbo Jumble®
$19.95 • ISBN: 978-1-57243-314-4

Jumble® Crosswords™

More than 175 puzzles!

Jumble® Crosswords™
$10.95 • ISBN: 978-1-57243-347-2